Praise for
31 Proverbs to Light Your Path

"Liz Curtis Higgs has a contagious passion for the Word of God, something you see so beautifully in play in *31 Proverbs to Light Your Path*. Practical, well-researched, and full of poignant stories, this book will empower you to live in light of God's wisdom."

—MARY DeMUTH, author of *Jesus Every Day*

"Truly a devotional treasure. In *31 Proverbs to Light Your Path*, Liz gently leads us through a series of proverbs, unpacking them with depth and insight as she shares discoveries from her own journey and offers ideas for personal application. This book reminds us that Proverbs is much more than a collection of pithy insights; it is a rich well of wisdom and revelation for everyday life. Keep it on your bedside table."

—Jo SAXTON, author of *The Dream of You* and board
chair of 3Dmovements

"With a delightfully fresh approach, *31 Proverbs to Light Your Path* illuminates familiar passages, and Liz makes the journey through these words of wisdom both personal and practical. Many books focus on general truths in Proverbs, but Liz goes word by word, and this digging turns up plenty of new treasures along the way. This is a book I'll gladly return to again and again."

—HOLLEY GERTH, author of *What Your Heart Needs
for the Hard Days*

"For most of my life, I've prayed one single prayer over and over: 'God, grant me wisdom!' Even as a child, I knew wisdom to be my lamp in the dark, a needed comfort while trying to find my way through a complicated life. In *31 Proverbs to Light Your Path*, Liz Curtis Higgs mines rich biblical text to reveal the brightest of lights, thirty-one truths with enough wattage to help you and me walk through the most difficult of nights. Even better, she comes alongside and takes the journey with us."

—MICHELE CUSHATT, author of *Undone* and *I Am*

"I absolutely love how Liz Curtis Higgs writes with clarity, tenderness, truth, humor, and depth. As in her other books, Liz uses careful study of God's Word to reveal the nuances of the original Hebrew in the selected scriptures. Formatted for both personal and group Bible study, this is not a read-only-once book. Each writing is full of richness that will have the reader discovering new insights with each reading. The "One Minute, One Step" challenges are practical, eye-opening, and sometimes convicting. You will come away from this book with a greater understanding of the character and goodness of God and how our lives can reflect His truth."

—VIVIAN MABUNI, author of *Warrior in Pink*

Praise for
31 Verses to Write on Your Heart

"Liz Curtis Higgs has given us a versatile resource. Part story-rich devotional and part study-driven commentary, *31 Verses to Write on Your Heart* is as smart as it is approachable, as profound as it is practical."

—AMANDA BIBLE WILLIAMS, Chief Content Officer of
She Reads Truth and coauthor of *Open Your Bible:
God's Word Is for You and for Now*

"Liz writes just as she speaks: eloquently, accurately, and with power. With her signature style, she weaves biblical context, fresh insight, and practical application in a way that empowers, educates, and equips. And if we ever needed a deeper understanding of God's Word, ever needed His precious truths written on our hearts, it's now. It's today."

—SUSIE LARSON, radio host of *Live the Promise*
and author of *Your Powerful Prayers*

"Consider *31 Verses to Write on Your Heart* your new spiritual strategy for deepening your daily walk with God. Full of relatable stories, this Scripture-saturated guide enables you to see familiar verses in a fresh, relevant way. Whether you've walked with Jesus for decades—or just since last Tuesday—this encouraging and practical book will fertilize your soul."

—KAREN EHMAN, Proverbs 31 Ministries national
speaker and *New York Times* best-selling author
of *Keep It Shut*

"Writing God's Word on our hearts is insurance. It's truth we can call on 24/7 in times of fear, insecurity, or intimidation. Liz, a faithful friend to all of us, has searched out truth and shared it by way of her brilliant mind and darling heart. Don't miss this chance for thirty-one days of life enrichment."

—PATSY CLAIRMONT, Women of Faith speaker, artist, and author of *You Are More Than You Know*

"Liz Curtis Higgs has a gift for taking important truths in Scripture and making them accessible, understandable, and easily digestible. You will be inspired and encouraged to cherish God's Word through practical and personal tips for hiding His letter of love in your heart."

—CHRYSTAL EVANS HURST, author of *She's Still There: Rescuing the Girl in You*

31 Proverbs
TO LIGHT YOUR
Path

Other Books by Liz Curtis Higgs

Nonfiction
Bad Girls of the Bible
Really Bad Girls of the Bible
Slightly Bad Girls of the Bible
Unveiling Mary Magdalene
Rise and Shine
Embrace Grace
My Heart's in the Lowlands
The Girl's Still Got It
It's Good to Be Queen
The Women of Christmas
The Women of Easter
31 Verses to Write on Your Heart

Contemporary Fiction
Mixed Signals
Bookends
Mercy Like Sunlight

Historical Fiction
Thorn in My Heart
Fair Is the Rose
Whence Came a Prince
Grace in Thine Eyes
Here Burns My Candle
Mine Is the Night
A Wreath of Snow

Children's
The Parable of the Lily
The Sunflower Parable
The Pumpkin Patch Parable
The Pine Tree Parable
Parable Treasury

LIZ CURTIS HIGGS

Best-selling author of *31 Verses to Write on Your Heart*

31 *Proverbs*
TO LIGHT YOUR
Path

WATERBROOK

31 Proverbs to Light Your Path

All Scripture quotations, unless otherwise indicated, are taken from the Holy Bible, New International Version®, NIV ®. Copyright © 1973, 1978, 1984, 2011 by Biblica Inc.® Used by permission. All rights reserved worldwide. For a list of the additional Bible versions that are quoted, see page 201.

Hardcover ISBN 978-1-60142-893-6
eBook ISBN 978-1-60142-894-3

Copyright © 2017 by Liz Curtis Higgs

Cover design and photography by Kelly L. Howard

Published in the United States by WaterBrook, an imprint of the Crown Publishing Group, a division of Penguin Random House LLC, New York.

WATERBROOK® and its deer colophon are registered trademarks of Penguin Random House LLC.

Library of Congress Cataloging-in-Publication Data
Names: Higgs, Liz Curtis, author.
Title: 31 proverbs to light your path / Liz Curtis Higgs.
Other titles: Thirty-one proverbs to light your path
Description: First Edition. | Colorado Springs : WaterBrook, 2017. | Includes bibliographi-
    cal references.
Identifiers: LCCN 2017026906| ISBN 9781601428936 (hardcover) | ISBN
    9781601428943 (electronic)
Subjects: LCSH: Bible. Proverbs—Meditations.
Classification: LCC BS1465.54 .H54 2017 | DDC 223/.706—dc23
LC record available at https://lccn.loc.gov/2017026906

Printed in the United States of America
2017—First Edition

10 9 8 7 6 5 4 3 2 1

SPECIAL SALES
Most WaterBrook books are available at special quantity discounts when purchased in bulk by corporations, organizations, and special-interest groups. Custom imprinting or excerpting can also be done to fit special needs. For information, please e-mail special marketscms@penguinrandomhouse.com or call 1-800-603-7051.

To my son, Matt,
my daughter, Lilly,
and my daughter-in-love, Beth:
The clear light you each shine on my path
brightens and widens my understanding of our world
and strengthens my grip on God's mercy.
For this and so much more,
I love you!
xox Mom

Contents

Walk with Me

When my physical therapist began our first session with "Quad sets are a neuromuscular isometric," I knew I was in trouble. He'd already lost me at "quad sets," which sounded like four games of tennis. But "neuromuscular isometric"?

"Seriously?" I blurted out, trying not to laugh.

His gaze narrowed. "Mrs. Higgs, do you plan on walking again?"

I sat up straighter in bed, wincing as pain ricocheted through my newly installed bionic knee. "Use all the big words you like. Just tell me what to do."

Following his instructions, I stretched out my leg, pointed my toes toward the ceiling, and slowly pressed the back of my knee into the bed. He counted while I held my muscles in place for ten seconds. After several repetitions I shrugged. "That's it? I barely moved."

"Good. Now ten more."

Once he assured me each rep would strengthen my knee and improve my range of motion, I stopped asking questions and started doing quad sets, ankle pumps, seated knee extensions, and all the other exercises on his clipboard. In due time I was mobile again, amazed at how a series of seemingly minor steps had carried me along the path to wellness.

Which brings me to you, to this book, to right now.

You and I will be walking step-by-step through thirty-one verses from the book of Proverbs. Left to my own devices, I might have picked only the upbeat verses, the cheerful ones. But when I asked hundreds of women to choose their favorites, they were wise enough to know that we learn more—and grow faster—when our thinking is challenged and our motives and actions are considered.

So as we look at the verses together, you'll likely find many are comforting, some are a bit unsettling, and a few may squash your toes, as they did mine. Yet you can be sure God crafted each word in Proverbs for your benefit, since He promises to "instruct you in the way of wisdom and lead you along straight paths."[1]

Clearly, God will do the leading. I'm here to keep you company.

We'll be taking a word-by-word-*by-word* approach to Bible study. My theory? Better to chew slowly and savor each phrase than to swallow a passage whole and not remember what we ate.

I've used more than thirty different English translations to capture the subtle nuances of the original Hebrew and enrich our understanding of His Word. If you're curious about notations such as ASV, which denotes the American Standard Version, you'll find a complete list of translations and their abbreviations on page

201. I've also included a Study Guide that further explores each chapter. You might answer the questions as you go, or you may decide to gather with a group of friends and use *31 Proverbs to Light Your Path* as a six-week Bible study.

At first glance the book of Proverbs appears to be a long list of rules about right living. More than one mom has thought about marching up to her teenager's bedroom door and demanding, "How long will you lie there, you sluggard?"[2] And more than one employee has been tempted to tell a coworker who peppers his speech with four-letter words, "Keep corrupt talk far from your lips."[3]

If you're looking for dos and don'ts, Proverbs has plenty to offer.

But the deeper truth it contains is *wisdom*. We'll discover why God calls us to righteousness and how He makes being good possible. We'll learn about our human nature and His divine nature, about the dark alleys to avoid and the well-lit paths to follow. God says of His Word, "This command is a lamp, this teaching is a light, and correction and instruction are the way to life."[4]

My goal is not to show you how to be good. My goal is to show you how good God is.

At the end of each chapter, I've added a simple challenge— "One Minute, One Step"—a do-it-now task that requires *sixty seconds or less*. If you have a notepad, a pen, a Bible, your purse, some stationery, and your phone, that's all you'll need. By moving straight from words to actions, we can immediately apply what we've learned and discover how God uses even the smallest steps to lead us in the right direction.

When you reach the "One Minute, One Step" prompt, I hope

you'll resist the urge to close the book, thinking, *Great idea! I'll try that later,* and instead just *do it.* Sixty seconds max, I promise. Think of it as a spiritual quad set—a tiny but powerful exercise to get you on your feet and on the move for God.

His light is shining, and the path ahead is clear. Ready when you are, beloved.

I

Morning by Morning

The path of the righteous is like the morning sun,
shining ever brighter till the full light of day.

PROVERBS 4:18

I rose earlier than usual one morning, nudged awake by two cats impatient for breakfast. The sky outside our kitchen window was a deep navy blue, the birdsong was lively, and the windowpanes were cold to the touch. As I gazed at the eastern horizon, the sky slowly grew lighter. If I watched without turning away, the change was too gradual to measure, but if I glanced down for a moment and then looked up, the difference was remarkable.

Our spiritual growth is much the same. Morning by morning we may not see any noticeable improvement in our thought patterns or behavior. But as we read God's Word, as we worship, as we pray, as we fellowship with other believers, as we serve Him with gladness, as we give away our resources to help others, the light of His love continues to rise in our hearts until it shows in our words and shines on our faces.

Now let's see what this verse from Proverbs has for us.

The path of the righteous . . . *Proverbs 4:18*

Very promising, the word *path*. God doesn't expect us to get where we're going all at once. This "road the righteous travel" (GNT), this "way of those who do right" (VOICE) is a pathway, not an expressway.

As to our being righteous, that is entirely the Lord's work. Righteousness isn't about our goodness; it's about God's goodness. We can't become "right-living people" (MSG) on our own. Our walk with Him is upright only because He bent down to carry a cross.

It's His Spirit in us that prompts us to say and do the right things—to be loving, joyful, peaceful, patient, kind, good, faithful, gentle, and disciplined.[1] All that delicious fruit of the Spirit is produced when we depend on God, not when we depend on our own strength. What a relief!

This is how our daily journey is meant to look and feel:

. . . is like the morning sun, . . . *Proverbs 4:18*

That "first gleam of dawn" (NLT), that "early morning light" (NLV) is not only pure; it's also sure. The sun never changes its mind, never chooses not to rise, never goes back to bed. It keeps moving, tracing a steady path across the sky. Even when threatening clouds hover over us, even when wild storms rage inside us, far above those thunderheads, the sun still shines.

Because of His power, we, too, can keep shining. Because of His Son, the light of the world, we can "glow" (MSG) despite our circumstances. We are still His people. He is still our God. Nothing will ever change that. Nothing.

You and I are counted among those who walk the path of the righteous, based not on how we act but on whom we follow. "The LORD is trustworthy in all he promises and faithful in all he does."[2] What He does is shine in us.

. . . shining ever brighter . . . Proverbs 4:18

He who created light and called it good also created you and called you righteous. You may be thinking, *That's fine, Liz, but life isn't "growing brighter and brighter" (EXB) at my house, and I'm definitely not feeling that my path is "clearer" (AMPC) with each passing day.*

I hear you. I'm with you. That's why God calls us to focus on truth. Rather than trust our ever-changing emotions, He wants us to trust what His Word tells us: "This righteousness is given through faith in Jesus Christ to all who believe."[3]

Do you believe, dear friend? Then count on God for the "brightening" (YLT) that is certain to appear. Don't look in the mirror. Look in His Word. See? It's coming.

. . . till the full light of day. Proverbs 4:18

Jesus promised, "Whoever follows me will never walk in darkness, but will have the light of life."[4] *His* light. *His* life. When do we reach "full light"? When we stand before His throne on that "perfect day" (ASV). Until then we live "in the ever-brightening light of God's favor" (TLB), with our faith expanding and our confidence strengthening.

By the very nature of the maturing process, we begin each day with more knowledge, more wisdom, and more experience than we had the day before. For those who love God, "the longer they live, the brighter they shine" (MSG). Why dread your next birthday when each year brings you closer to the One who loves you more than anyone on earth ever could?

A glorious day will come—just imagine it!—when we say with our faces lifted in awe, "Good morning, Lord." May the anticipation of that joyous moment propel us forward on our path, knowing we are moving in the right direction: toward Him.

Lord Jesus,
help me turn away from darkness,
disappointment, and discouragement
to gaze steadily at You,
my Source of light and life,
my sun and my shield.
Strengthen my trust in You
for the big things, for the small things,
for all things.
Remind me that, as sure as the sun
rises every morning,
Your goodness and righteousness
will shine on me and in me,
morning by morning,
brighter and brighter.

One Minute, One Step

Invite more light into your life.

Look around for an easy way to brighten your immediate surroundings. Open a curtain, pull up a window blind, or maybe turn on more lights. You might try dusting a light bulb you can easily reach. The lamp should be turned off and the bulb cool. Carefully wipe it clean with a soft cloth or dryer sheet, and then turn on the lamp. Surprise! A significant difference, yes?

Now that you've added more light, what do you see that you didn't notice before?

The path of the righteous is like the morning sun,
shining ever brighter till the full light of day.

PROVERBS 4:18

2

Wisdom's Source

For the LORD gives wisdom;
from his mouth come knowledge and understanding.

PROVERBS 2:6

*W*ant to know the best restaurant in town? Consult a bona fide foodie. Need a different hair stylist? Ask a friend with a fabulous cut. Time to get a new camera? Check with a seasoned photographer.

When we want solutions for life's basic questions, we have resources all around us. But when our hearts ache for something we can't even name, there is only one place to turn.

For the LORD gives wisdom; . . . *Proverbs 2:6*

People are quick to hand out opinions—"I think this" or "I believe that"—and if they're experts, they may charge a fee. But when God speaks to our hearts, we know He's "the source" (ERV) of all truth, and He "gives out Wisdom free" (MSG).

Free. Let that sink in for a moment. *Free* is as generous as it gets.

When we buy a Bible—His words, His truth—we are paying for the translating and the proofreading, the printing and the binding, but the priceless wisdom on those pages is ours for the taking. "For the LORD grants wisdom!" (NLT). He gives away the deepest secrets of the universe and shares with those He loves His "skillful and godly Wisdom" (AMPC).

If we spent countless dollars and the whole of our lives trying to read every book on every shelf, we still wouldn't have what God offers us at no charge.

... from his mouth come ... *Proverbs 2:6*

He spoke into existence the world and all it contains. "And God said, 'Let there be light,' and there was light."[1] He is still speaking. He has never stopped speaking. His wisdom falls on us like rain from the heavens, watering our souls so they bear much fruit. God declares, "The words I speak are like that. They will not return to me without producing results. They will accomplish what I want them to. They will do exactly what I sent them to do."[2]

His Word not only pours out of God's mouth; it's also meant to pour out of our mouths, especially if we teach the Bible. Someday when I work up the courage, I'm going to stand in front of an audience and simply read the Word of God without adding a single word of my own. No humorous asides, no personal stories, no quotes from the Lizzie Revised Version. Just the truth of Scripture, proclaimed with all the passion and excitement it deserves.

Think what could happen if we got out of the way and let God's Word go forth, trusting its ability to transform those who hear it. Sister, just the idea makes me want to stand up and shout!

How God longs for us to grasp the treasure He offers.

. . . knowledge and understanding. Proverbs 2:6

Knowledge is power, all right—the power of God, the One who knows everything.

Donald Rumsfeld, a former US secretary of defense, made this classic statement about knowledge: "As we know, there are known knowns; there are things we know we know. We also know there are known unknowns; that is to say we know there are some things we do not know. But there are also unknown unknowns— the ones we don't know we don't know."[3]

Unknown unknowns? People are still shaking their heads over that one.

But there truly *are* things we don't know we don't know. And those things? God knows them all. He tells us, "As the heavens are higher than the earth, so are my ways higher than your ways and my thoughts than your thoughts."[4]

When we throw up our hands and say, "I don't get it, Lord," He says, "Exactly."

I'm grateful God gets what we don't get, knows what we don't know, and loves us right where we are. His "true knowledge and insight" (voice), His "prudence" (dra), His "intelligence" (jub) stretch far beyond the stars, yet He graciously shares them with His children. This is a God who cares about everything that matters to us, who sees our deepest needs and meets them with the one thing He knows will make a difference: His wisdom.

That thing we think is too small, too insignificant for God's attention? He not only cares about it; He also knows what to do about it. Friends may offer sympathy, a tissue, a listening ear, but God brings us what we really need. "If any of you lacks wisdom, you should ask God, who gives generously to all without finding fault, and it will be given to you."[5]

Freely given without judgment, to be freely received without shame.

Wisdom, knowledge, and *understanding* are three separate words in the original Hebrew, each one suggesting a deeper meaning than simply information. All three can be gained by spending time in God's Word as a priority, not as an afterthought squeezed in between reading e-mails and pulling a bagel out of the toaster oven. On those mornings when I hurry past my Bible, whispering some "Sorry, but I'm kinda busy" excuse, the Lord tugs at my conscience, drawing me back. Not with guilt, but with love.

Come and sit with Me, Liz. Let's read My Word together.

Who could refuse such a tender invitation? When I join Him at our old library table, with its cracked oak veneer and scuffed legs, there's nowhere I would rather be and nothing I would rather do than open His Word and learn from the Master.

Can I see Him? No. Can I sense His nearness? Oh yes.

The Bible in front of me is three decades old and looks it. The pages are covered with scribbled notations, underlined words, and the occasional coffee stain. Pen in hand, I add a new note in the margin, perhaps date it, and then thank God for what He has kindly shown me.

This kind of higher education isn't for some of us. It's for all of us. There are no exams, no grades, and the tuition is paid in full. Just come.

Heavenly Father,
forgive me when I take Your wisdom,
Your knowledge, and Your understanding
for granted.
Let me wake each morning with a deep hunger
that no breakfast can satisfy.
Woo me to Your side,
and teach me Your Word.
Fill my mind, heart, and soul
with Your marvelous truth.

One Minute, One Step

Listen to the sound of wisdom.

Read aloud Psalm 139:1–14, letting each beautiful verse sink in as you hear His Word spoken in your voice. God wrote these words about you and for you. He has searched you and knows you. He is always with you and will always guide you. Because He made you, you are wonderful.

This is God's Word for you. This is truth.

For the LORD gives wisdom;
from his mouth come knowledge and understanding.

PROVERBS 2:6

3

Weigh In

A person may think their own ways are right,
but the LORD weighs the heart.

PROVERBS 21:2

I meant well. That's what I tell myself when I've done the wrong thing for the supposed right reason—or the right thing for the altogether wrong reason. Either way, I've messed up and am trying to justify my actions. That's why the last verse in the book of Judges always makes me wince, because it sums up our twisted way of thinking: "everyone did what was right in his own eyes."[1] Busted.

Whenever we take our focus away from God's wisdom, it's easy to veer off in the wrong direction, convincing ourselves we know what's best. We say things like this:

"It's my life. Don't I deserve to be happy?"

"This is how I relax. I'm not hurting anyone."

"Hey, at least I haven't broken one of the Ten Commandments!"

Believe me, I've used all those excuses and dozens more. Not one of them honors the Lord, which is why this verse is worth a closer look.

A person may think . . . *Proverbs 21:2*

Some translations say "man" (ESV), but clearly this is an equal-opportunity challenge for "everyone" (VOICE), male or female, old or young. We're all guilty of filtering what's right and wrong through our "own view" (CJB), our "own eyes" (ASV). What seems straightforward to us may appear very crooked to the Lord.

. . . their own ways are right, . . .
Proverbs 21:2

From our viewpoint our "path is straight" (CEB), so we tell ourselves we're "doing the right thing" (CEV). But the more we have to convince ourselves and "justify our every deed" (TLB), the more likely we're doing something wrong.

When it comes to judging ourselves and our actions, we're hardly disinterested parties. We're partial. We want to be good, perhaps even do good, and if at all possible *look* good doing it. When our methods don't line up with God's Word, though, we may find ourselves on a dead-end street, wondering how we got there.

. . . but . . . *Proverbs 21:2*

Of the thirty-one proverbs in this book, thirteen have the word *but* right in the middle. Like a hinged door, *but* leads to another possibility or an important comparison. *But* can also serve as a flashing light, a warning, a stop sign.

But halts our wayward thinking and puts us back on track.

But forces us to reconsider and reminds us who is in charge.

Whatever we may convince ourselves is right, God calls us to "remember" (GNT) that He sees who we truly are. "This is how we know that we belong to the truth and how we set our hearts at rest in his presence: If our hearts condemn us, we know that God is greater than our hearts, and he knows everything."[2] Yes, He does.

Our hearts are His dwelling place, His permanent home. God doesn't perch on our shoulders or nip at our ankles or circle our heads like a halo. He lives in our hearts, and so does His Word. "Sharper than any double-edged sword, it penetrates even to dividing soul and spirit, joints and marrow; it judges the thoughts and attitudes of the heart."[3]

No one knows the home you live in better than you do. The door that sticks, the step that creaks, the cabinets that aren't quite straight, the thin spots in the carpet, the shower tiles that need caulking. You know what your current living space is worth and what it would take to make it perfect.

God knows all that and more about your heart. He has taken a careful assessment, having measured the width of your mercy and the depth of your compassion.

> . . . the LORD weighs the heart. *Proverbs 21:2*

This is not our literal hearts, beating in our chests, but our spiritual hearts, hidden to all but the Lord, who "examines" (NLT) and "evaluates" (HCSB). He knows the "motives" (TLB) and "reasons" (NCV) behind our thoughts, words, and actions. There's no point trying to mask our true intentions when our hearts are ever on display for His inspection. God "always knows what is in our hearts" (CEV), and He's fully aware of what He'll find there.

If we have the Holy Spirit, we can count on God to prod our hearts anytime we're doing something that's just plain wrong. He has every right to do so, because He loves us unconditionally and sacrificially and because we've pledged our lives to Him.

For years whenever I passed panhandlers on the street, I looked the other way, telling myself that if I gave them money, they would waste it on alcohol or drugs or worse. The ugly truth was, I didn't want to part with my cash. Uglier still, I didn't think the person deserved it. This from a beggar of grace who deserved nothing and received everything.

Finally one verse pierced my heart like an arrow: "Truly I tell you, whatever you did not do for one of the least of these, you did not do for me."[4] *Oh, Jesus.* Was that You sitting outside the grocery store, hunger in Your eyes? Standing near an intersection, holding a battered sign?

It *was* Him. It *is* Him.

Jesus asks us to love, not judge. To meet people's gaze, not look away. To be generous, not selfish. To say, "This is a gift from the Lord," because it is. To trust Him with how the money is spent and to give without hesitation or regret.

Though our hearts may have been "weighed on the scales and found wanting,"[5] the One who knows us best cleanses our hearts of all unrighteousness and fills them with His love. When we're no longer full of ourselves, we have far more room for Him.

Heavenly Father,
renew my mind and reshape my motives.
Make my crooked paths straight.
Teach my heart to beat with Yours.
Keep me from calling right things wrong
and wrong things right.
Forgive me when I fail, Lord.
Weigh me with Your scale called Grace.

One Minute, One Step

***

Reach for your wallet.

Take out some cash, as much as you can spare. Slip the money inside an envelope, seal it, and then tuck it into your glove compartment or a zippered pocket of your purse. Ask God to show you who needs this money more than you do.

That's the sixty-second part. Now watch and wait in the days to come.

God may point you to a harried mother counting out her loose change in the checkout line at a grocery store or an elderly woman sitting on a park bench wearing tattered clothes. When God nudges you, quietly put the envelope in her hands and tell her it's a gift from the One who made her and loves her. Expect nothing in return, not even gratitude. Smile and move on.

Now resist the urge to tell anyone. Ever. Let this be just between you and the Lord.

A person may think their own ways are right,
but the LORD weighs the heart.

PROVERBS 21:2

4

Cover Up

Hatred stirs up conflict,
but love covers over all wrongs.

PROVERBS 10:12

*H*ate isn't a word we often use at the Higgs house, though when our kids were little, they each got to pick one "hate food"—something we promised never to put on their plates or ask them to eat. Our son hated carrots. Our daughter, potatoes. (Now that they're adults, I'm happy to report both items are back on the menu.)

But hating people? Not an option. In fact, we're called to do just the opposite. "Dear friends, since God so loved us, we also ought to love one another."[1] Loving people isn't always easy, but it's always possible. Our verse today points the way.

Hatred stirs up . . . *Proverbs 10:12*

This kind of hatred goes beyond mere emotion. It's a cruel word that's spoken or a spiteful action that's taken. It's a force of energy that "fuels" (VOICE) our anger and "causes" (ERV) us to say or do things we wish we'd never said or done. The Hebrew word translated "stirs up" literally means to "rouse" or "awaken."[2] That's exactly what hatred feels like—a sleeping monster coming to life inside us.

What's the source of our ill will toward others, however fleeting? In my experience it usually boils down to fear. Fear of being overlooked, ignored, discounted. Fear of harm coming to us or those we love. Fear of being taken advantage of. Fear of our lives spiraling out of control.

When fear is awakened, we sometimes lash out, speaking without thinking, which leads to the inevitable.

... conflict, ... *Proverbs 10:12*

In fiction conflict is a good thing. It keeps the reader turning pages, eager to see what happens next. But in real life "trouble" (CEV) isn't a pleasant pastime, and "strife" (ESV) is bound to ruin our day. No one wants to work at a job or live in a house filled with "disputes" (CJB) and "arguments" (ERV).

We may manage to keep a lid on our emotions when we're with friends, family, or coworkers because so much is at stake, and we can't risk losing those crucial relationships. But let a stranger take offense at our choices or beliefs, and we may find ourselves embroiled in a verbal or online battle with painful consequences. "They sharpen their tongues like swords and aim cruel words like deadly arrows."[3] *Ouch.*

God knows how easily we can be drawn into conflict, which is why He offers us a way out. An uplifting option. A much-needed recourse.

... but love ... *Proverbs 10:12*

This love is born from God's love for us. It's "charity" (DRA) in the deepest sense. It's caring about others, whether friends or foes. It's genuine compassion.

The best description of this kind of love? "It does not dishonor others, it is not self-seeking, it is not easily angered, it keeps no record of wrongs."[4] On my best days I wouldn't dream of doing any of that stuff. On my worst days I'm capable of doing all that stuff, especially the self-seeking bit. When I find myself asking questions like "What's in it for me?" or "How will this benefit me?" or "Why does this always happen to me?" then I know I'm off the mark.

What's a foolish sinner to do? Throw herself at the mercy of God, who pours His perfect love on imperfect us, drowning our sins in the ocean of His grace.

... covers over ... *Proverbs 10:12*

God's love for His people makes our love for others possible. Love "overlooks" (CEV) instead of looking down with disdain. Love "calms" (VOICE) rather than agitates. Love "forgives" (GNT) even as it fortifies. This kind of love "always protects, always trusts, always hopes, always perseveres,"[5] pressing beyond our changeable moods to offer mercy to a hurting world. The original Greek word translated "covers" means "clothes, conceals, hides."

Love blankets the hatred, the hurt, the humiliation. As The Message paraphrases it, "love pulls a quilt over the bickering."

. . . all wrongs. *Proverbs 10:12*

That word *all* sums things up, friend. When love is in the house, "transgressions" (ASV) are forgotten and "offenses" (CEB) are undone. Even "insults" (TLB) lose their sting and "rebellions" (VOICE) are quashed.

Because Jesus blots out our sins, we can extend His grace to others. No wonder we find an echo of Proverbs 10:12 in the New Testament: "Above all, love each other deeply, because love covers over a multitude of sins."[6]

Lord Jesus,
I'm grateful You see me
and even more grateful You love me.
When I feel unseen, unwanted,
unnecessary, unloved,
help me get my eyes off myself
and focus my attention on others,
forgiving them as You forgive me.
In a world full of hatred,
let me always carry Your banner of love.

One Minute, One Step

Learning to love again.

Write down the name of someone who has wounded or offended you, along with a few details—when it happened, where it happened, and what happened. Holding the record of that painful memory in your hands, pray for the strength to forgive this person, even if he or she hasn't asked for forgiveness and likely never will.

Now tear up the paper and drop it piece by piece into a wastebasket. Let the healing begin.

Hatred stirs up conflict,
but love covers over all wrongs.

PROVERBS 10:12

5

No Telling

A gossip betrays a confidence,
but a trustworthy person keeps a secret.

PROVERBS 11:13

You're hanging out with friends. Sharing a meal, sharing your lives. Someone's name comes up. Someone who isn't there.

A comment is made. "Have you seen _____?" Then another. "Well, I heard _____."

Once people realize you know the person they're talking about better than anyone else at the table, heads turn in your direction. Faces look at you expectantly. What happens next depends on how willing you are to honor this proverb and the One who wrote it.

This isn't about heaping guilt on your shoulders or mine. This is about God setting us free from the sin that binds us.

A gossip . . . *Proverbs 11:13*

We often think of *gossip* as a verb—something we do. But here it's a noun—something we are. The kind of person who "can't keep secrets" (NCV), who likes to "talk about others" (NIrV) and is "always telling stories" (NLV).

Gossip is often fueled by a desperate need for attention. *Look at me. Listen to me. I know a secret. I must be special.*

A busybody often has a busy body, carrying the news hither and yon. Once this "gadabout gossip" (MSG) hears some juicy tidbit, she "walketh deceitfully" (DRA) and "goeth guilefully" (WYC), putting not only her mouth in motion but also her feet. Even in the computer age, gossips are more likely to spill the beans in person rather than risk a cyber trail. An e-mail or text is easily traced, but spoken words are lost to the winds.

Besides, half the thrill of telling tales is seeing how people respond to the news. (I wish I didn't know that, but I do.)

. . . betrays a confidence, . . . *Proverbs 11:13*

And what a cruel betrayal it is when a gossip "makes secrets known" (NLV). How many friendships have been destroyed, marriages torn apart, and businesses ruined by an idle word, a whispered rumor, a secret that's no longer a secret?

For some of us this sort of behavior isn't even a temptation, let alone a common practice. We wouldn't dream of wounding a friend or betraying another's trust. When we say, "Your secret is safe with me," we mean it. If you beg us, "Don't tell anyone," we don't. My friend Rebecca is like this; a coworker called her "The Vault."

But others among us feel uncomfortable when the topic of

gossip comes up. Frankly, we enjoy passing along some interesting story we've heard. We don't consider ourselves heartless or thoughtless—just curious and gregarious. What we see, we share. What we discover, we uncover. If we promise not to tell, we won't, but if no such promise is made, we convince ourselves we mean no harm.

Only you and the Lord know which description fits you. I confess, I fall in both camps: totally zipped lips with the big stuff that truly matters, less careful with the small stuff that seems insignificant but really isn't.

For all who walk in victory, praise God. For those of us who struggle, here's the help we need.

. . . but a trustworthy person . . . Proverbs 11:13

It's what we all long to be, every one of us. A "true friend" (CEV) with a "faithful heart" (GNV). A "reliable person" (VOICE) and "someone of integrity" (MSG). The original Hebrew means "confirm, support." That's the job of every believer. To build up rather than tear down. To stand beside, not stand in judgment. To protect instead of expose.

. . . keeps a secret. Proverbs 11:13

Even if talking about others is deeply ingrained in our nature, God is able to change us through the transforming power of the Holy Spirit, who provides the strength we need. He offers edifying words we can and should say and keeps us from sharing private confidences meant for our ears alone. Thanks to the Spirit's power, we can become a trustworthy friend who "conceals the matter" (JUB) and "won't violate a confidence" (MSG).

Alas, it took me a long time to learn this.

In my early years of writing and speaking, my favorite stories were about my kids. Some incidents were funny, others tender, and all were real-life relatable. How could I go wrong? I'll tell you how—by not asking my children's permission to share them.

After an especially bad day at school, our daughter, who was ten at the time, posted a handwritten sign on her bedroom door that urged us to STAY OUT, including a list of reasons that were (I confess) highly amusing. Always grateful for new material, I laminated her sign and stuck it in the binder with my speaking notes. Audiences loved the story, and it was great fun to share—until the day Lilly found her sign in my binder.

"Mom!" Her eyes widened in dismay. "Why did you save this? And why is it in *here*?"

My face grew hot with shame. What could I say? That I'd told thousands of people about her bad day at school and her funny way of handling it? Even though I always ended the story on a sweet note, with her snuggled in my arms, nothing could erase the sad truth that I'd shared her words without asking if I could.

I apologized profusely. Begged her forgiveness. And learned a valuable (and humbling) lesson. Loose lips sink relationships. Trust is the buoy that keeps them afloat.

P.S. Did I ask my grown daughter to read and approve this chapter before it went to print? You bet. I may be a slow learner, but God made certain this lesson stuck.

Heavenly Father,
help me see "sharing" for what it truly is:
thoughtless, careless, pointless gossip.
Forgive me.
Guide me.
Lock my lips, and set me free.

One Minute, One Step

Become a secret keeper.

Think of something recently shared with you in confidence. Silently pray for this person, mentally recounting in detail everything you know rather than saying it aloud or writing it down. Now that you've relieved your desire to tell someone by telling the Lord, leave this secret safely in His hands.

A gossip betrays a confidence,
but a trustworthy person keeps a secret.

PROVERBS 11:13

6

We All Fall Down

Pride goes before destruction,
a haughty spirit before a fall.

PROVERBS 16:18

The kind of pride that gets us into trouble stems from vanity, hubris, conceit. Thinking *I've got this* when we clearly don't. Saying "No thanks" when we really need help. Seeing humility as weakness. Letting an inflated ego get in the way of common sense.

When pride goes unchecked, it can send us tumbling.

Pride goes before destruction, . . . *Proverbs 16:18*

The Lord doesn't say pride sometimes ends badly. No, it's a guaranteed outcome. "If you are proud, you will be destroyed"

(NIrV). *A* always leads to *B*. "First pride, then the crash" (MSG). Pride is "the first step" (ERV) down the wrong path, the one that leads to "disaster" (CEB).

> . . . a haughty spirit before a fall.
> *Proverbs 16:18*

Pride begins with "arrogance" (GNT) and results in "failure" (CJB) every time. I remember one such time in particular. Oh baby.

After speaking at a conference in Cape Town, South Africa, I had to fly to Johannesburg before boarding my eighteen-hour flight home. The discount airline—their motto was "More nice, less price"—permitted just one checked bag weighing no more than forty pounds. That meant my carry-on, jammed with books, weighed a *ton*.

When we landed and prepared to disembark, the crew didn't wave those of us seated in the back of the plane to move forward toward the Jetway. No, no. Instead, they pointed to a long, flimsy set of stairs leading from the back of our big plane down to the tarmac ten feet below. It was more of an emergency exit. No railing, no sides, no kidding.

I took two steps down before the male flight attendant waiting at the bottom saw my dilemma and started up, his hand outstretched to take my overstuffed bag.

A smart woman would have stopped at that point and waited for help. An even smarter woman would have asked for assistance before starting down. But a foolish, prideful woman thinks, *I can handle this myself,* and takes one more step.

Over the side I went, heavy bag still in hand, plunging toward the ground headfirst. My thoughts at that moment were concise. *This is it. This is how I die.*

Seconds later I landed with a sickening thud. Then a wave of shock washed over me, followed by amazement. I was *alive.* I had *survived.* Still lying on the tarmac, I did a quick head-to-toe check and was relieved to find I could move my head and neck, my shoulders and back, my thighs and knees. *Thank You, Lord.*

A glance at my hands revealed one minor injury. A thumbnail was torn to the quick, leaving a jagged edge. Since someone would need to help me get up and might get stabbed in the process, I reached inside my purse for an emery board.

That's when I saw our worship leader standing at the bottom of the stairs with a look of horror on her face. "*Liz!* What are you doing?!"

"Filing my nail," I explained, as if I hadn't a care in the world.

"You . . . you . . . *fell!*" she sputtered, hurrying to my side. "Are you okay?"

"I think so." But when I tried to sit up, a sharp pain shot through my right foot, still trapped beneath my bag. It took three people to help me stand and a wheelchair to roll me inside the terminal. The airport medic gave my foot a once-over, wrapped it in an Ace bandage, and sent me on my way, assuring me that my foot wasn't broken.

After a long, pain-racked flight home, I hobbled into my husband's embrace, glad I'd decided not to call him from South Africa. What would I have said? "Hi, honey! I fell out of an airplane . . ."

Three days later the burning pain and swelling had grown

worse. Three doctors later a diagnosis was made. My bones and muscles were fine, but the nerves in my foot were not.

"This could go one of two ways," the doctor explained. "You will either have unremitting pain with crippling, irreversible changes, or you could experience spontaneous remission." Surely *spontaneous remission* was the medical term for *miracle*.

When I looked up my symptoms on the Internet (not recommended), I learned that some patients with this condition end up in a wheelchair, and amputation might be necessary.

Say *what?*

In the days that followed, I prayed like mad and did what I was told, attaching electrodes to my seemingly frozen foot and trying to wiggle my toes. God, in His infinite kindness, answered my prayers. By the end of the summer, I could stand without wincing, walk without crying, and approach a flight of stairs without having a meltdown.

If I'd just let go of that carry-on bag, I would have been injury-free except for some colorful bruises. But I didn't let go. I hung on tightly, not only to my hand luggage, but also to my pride. God's Word makes it plain that "a proud attitude brings ruin" (EXB) and "an arrogant spirit gives way to a nasty fall" (VOICE).

My three crooked toes are a permanent reminder of that truth. So are these three lessons I learned about being humble instead of prideful:

Ask for assistance when it's needed.

Accept help when it's offered.

And thank God for small miracles.

Bless You, Lord,
for sparing my life.
Please forgive my foolish pride,
my stubborn attitude,
and my unwillingness to admit
I need help.
I am grateful for Your kindness
and even more thankful
for Your boundless patience.

One Minute, One Step

～❦～

**Put aside your pride and
ask for what you need.**

Write down an important task you must do this week
that's difficult for you to manage alone, either because you
don't possess the physical strength or because you don't
have the know-how to do the job well. Next to that task
note the names of one or two people who could help you
and how best to reach them. Decide what time today you'll
contact them. Sooner is better. Maybe right now?

*Pride goes before destruction,
a haughty spirit before a fall.*

PROVERBS 16:18

7

With This Ring

*Her husband has full confidence in her
and lacks nothing of value.*

PROVERBS 31:11

I didn't marry until I was almost thirty-two, so I had plenty of time to consider what kind of guy would make a great husband. "Tall, dark, and handsome" barely made the list. My top five? "Honest, joyful, confident, flexible," and, above all, "a man after God's own heart."

When I met my Bill, I discovered he has all those fine qualities in abundance. (The fact that he's tall, *silver,* and handsome is a bonus.) I soon found out what he was looking for in a wife. At the top of his list? A woman he could trust completely.

Uh-oh.

If you're not married and are tempted to take a pass on this proverb, here's something to consider. When a woman focuses on becoming the kind of person she'd want to marry—thoughtful, loving, sincere, faithful—she's more likely to attract a man who admires the same qualities. If that guy never comes along? Or if you're not planning to marry? Then you'll end up being an amazing, godly woman who pleases the One who loves you most.

Whatever your marital status, I promise this one's for you.

Her husband has full confidence in her . . .
Proverbs 31:11

Full confidence. As in 100 percent. The kind of woman that a man "relies on and believes in" (AMPC). All the time. In every situation. When her husband "entrusts his heart to her" (CEB), he does so willingly, knowing she has offered her heart in return.

Still, it may take a few turns of the calendar before a husband trusts his wife "without reserve" (MSG). After all, you can fall in love, but you can't fall in trust. Trust doesn't come from romantic dinners and kisses on the doorstep. Trust, unlike love, is not blind. Trust is based on time, experience, and year-in, year-out faithfulness.

After more than three decades of marriage, I can confidently say Bill and I trust each other fully. In particular, Bill trusts me with his heart, his emotional center. As his best friend, I know all his tender spots, pressure points, and fault lines, and I keep them well guarded.

He has also learned to trust me with our money. This took a little longer.

. . . and lacks nothing of value. *Proverbs 31:11*

The Hebrew word translated "value" means "spoil, plunder, booty." So a husband with a trustworthy wife has "no need for robbery" (WYC) or "[dishonest] spoil" (AMPC). He doesn't have to buy lottery tickets, hoping to cover the Visa bill, and he "will never be poor" (ERV) because of his wife's careless spending.

The Lord tested my trustworthiness in this area even before Bill and I married. There we were on a wintry weeknight, shopping for my engagement ring. The salesclerk smiled as we gingerly touched the loose diamonds she'd strewn across a square of blue velvet. "What's your budget?" she asked, her tone hopeful.

Bill gulped. "Four hundred." On a college teacher's salary, it was all he could afford, but I still winced when he said it. Four hundred dollars meant a very small diamond. Tiny. Except for the flaws. Those would be huge.

The salesclerk guided us to the other end of the counter. "I think we can find something here that will suit you." Out came another velvet square. The diamond chips she placed on it nearly disappeared in the nap of the fabric.

Bill listened as she explained clarity and carat weight, while my gaze drifted back to the larger stones still on display. Their many facets caught the bright store lights, winking at me, beckoning me.

Diamonds are forever, I told myself. Surely there was a way we could swing something larger. When no solution came to mind, I chose a pretty but petite gemstone and tried my best to be excited.

Bill touched my elbow. "Make sure you're happy with it, Liz, while I look around."

I was happy with Bill, no question. The dearest of men, generous and kind. But was I delighted with a diminutive diamond? *Hmmm.* As a single woman I'd grown accustomed to buying whatever I wanted, even if that meant pulling out my credit card.

My frugal fiancé, though, was a cash-and-carry kind of guy. Still, he *did* say he wanted me to be happy . . .

I waited until Bill was out of earshot before I leaned over the counter, waving the clerk closer. "Could I look at the bigger stones again?"

She placed them in front of me without a word. "I really like this one," I whispered, eyeing a square-cut beauty. "Suppose Bill gave you a check for four hundred dollars and I slipped you a check for the difference?"

She looked at me evenly. "Are you sure this is how you want to begin your marriage?"

Heat flew to my cheeks. "No, I . . . uh . . . guess not." I quickly turned away, ashamed to have my sins spread out like so many finely cut stones. Greed, deceit, covetousness, pride—it was not a pretty sight.

Today's verse from Proverbs 31, long ago committed to memory, sprang to mind right when I needed it most. "The heart of her husband trusts in her" (NASB). From across the room I studied Bill, a man who deserved a woman he could trust with his heart *and* his wallet, and silently begged his forgiveness for even considering such a thing.

The salesclerk was right. That was not how I wanted to begin my married life. Thank goodness I'd just been handed something more valuable than diamonds: a second chance. When I turned back to her, we both were smiling. "The smaller stone will be perfect," I assured her. And it was.

As the years have gone by, I've flashed my ring as if it were the Hope Diamond, because for me that's what it represents: hope for a marriage built on honesty, not deception, and a forever kind of love that outshines any sparkling gem.

Lord Jesus,
thank You for providing
gentle but firm words of correction
when I need them most.
Help me be a trustworthy woman
all the days of my life
for the sake of those I love
and even more
for Your name's sake.

One Minute, One Step

✦✦✦

Recognize the value of even the smallest things.

Slip off any jewelry you might be wearing, or find a favorite piece, and give it a good cleaning. For silver, gold, or gemstones (but *not* pearls or opals), squirt some liquid soap in your hands and gently rub the piece. Then rinse it with clear water and polish it dry with a soft towel. If your jewelry is made of leather, wood, or plastic, a slightly damp towel will take care of any dust or grime.

While your hands are busy, think of the story behind the jewelry. If it was a gift, take a moment to pray for the giver. If you bought it for yourself, consider what made it worth the investment, however large or small.

Her husband has full confidence in her
and lacks nothing of value.

PROVERBS 31:11

8

Bloom On

*The fruit of the righteous is a tree of life,
and the one who is wise saves lives.*

PROVERBS 11:30

My gardening skills are nil. I forget what I planted and where I planted it. Each spring when my bulbs burst into bloom, I'm surprised all over again. I'm also reminded of how little I've done—basically pushed them into the ground—and how much God has done. He created the seeds and the soil, watered them with rain, bathed them with sunlight, and then coaxed the first green shoots through the remains of last autumn's mulch.

Always God. Only God.

The same God who moves mountains and oceans also moves in our hearts, growing us into the image of His Son with the goal of producing healthy fruit.

The fruit of the righteous . . . *Proverbs 11:30*

Because of God's grace, we are counted as righteous. Because of His Son, "the seeds of good deeds" (NLT) are planted in us and bear fruit. We "live right" (CEV) when Christ lives in us. That means "the fruit that godly people bear" (NIrV) is wholly dependent on God, not on our meager gardening abilities. Because of His loving-kindness, God plants His righteousness inside us so that a bold new life breaks through.

. . . is a tree of life, . . . Proverbs 11:30

What does this "tree that bears life-giving fruit" (TLB) look like in real life? Like a mother who reads from a children's Bible to the little one squirming in her lap because she knows the Word contains truth and life. Like a father who hoes and weeds a garden with his children by his side, teaching them the biblical principles of seedtime and harvest. Like a coworker who loves God and communicates that love daily to everyone who crosses her path. Like a friend who cares about what you care about and believes "a good person gives life to others" (NCV). Like a senior saint who continues to teach Sunday school or collect the offering or greet newcomers, standing on the promise "They will still bear fruit in old age, they will stay fresh and green."[1]

Good fruit comes from good trees, and good trees come from good seeds. "The tree of life grows where the fruit of right-living falls" (VOICE). If we manage to do something right, it may come as a surprise to us, but it's never a surprise to God. He plants, waters, and nurtures us with His Word. In due season something beautiful will appear.

. . . and the one who is wise . . . Proverbs 11:30

That's the book of Proverbs for you. It's all about gaining wisdom—wisdom *from* God and wisdom *about* God. Not so we can be wisenheimers, but so that when we "act wisely, others will follow" (CEV). As the psalmist said, we'll be "like a tree planted by streams of water, which yields its fruit in season."[2]

Maybe you're a bloom-where-you're-planted kind of woman. You've stayed grounded in your proven gifts, content with slow but steady growth. Season after season God has faithfully added nutrients to the soil around your roots and has watered and pruned and fertilized and mulched. Certain of your calling, you've sensed the warmth of His pleasure, like sunlight pouring across your shoulders on a late spring afternoon.

But sometimes God calls us to bloom where we've been *transplanted* for the sake of others. Maybe you've felt a certain restlessness stirring inside, like roots cramped in a too-small pot. You have a deep longing to do more for God—something scarier, something riskier. When friends talk about serving Him in radically different ways, you lean in, wondering if God might be tugging at your well-established roots, preparing to lift you out of the familiar and replant you where you can truly flourish.

Grow here, dear child. I prepared this soil especially for you.

To sort out if it's time to stretch our branches, we need to ask ourselves if our desire for growth is based on coveting or on calling? Do we want what someone else has, or do we want to go wherever God might plant us, even if it means moving to a weed-infested section of the garden or to a quieter corner?

God alone is the Master Gardener, and He manages our lives according to His divine design. "I, the LORD, bring down the tall tree and raise up the lowly tree, and make the green tree wither and the dry tree bloom."[3]

Rather than charging ahead, we can study the Scriptures and pray until He makes the way clear. As Jesus told His disciples, "The seed on good soil stands for those with a noble and good heart, who hear the word, retain it, and by persevering produce a crop."[4] It's the persevering part that's often the hardest, yet it's also the most important. By waiting we learn patience. By praying we discover peace. Who doesn't need more of both?

. . . saves lives. *Proverbs 11:30*

If you've had the honor of watching someone step into God's kingdom, then you know why "those who are wise give new life to others" (ERV). But let me make this clear: We don't lead people to Christ. He draws them to Himself while we cheer from the sidelines.

Nothing is more thrilling than seeing the first glimmer of grace transform someone's face. No wonder God calls *wise* the one who "wins souls" (CJB), who "teaches others how to live" (NCV). The Hebrew word for "lives" here means "a soul, a living being." That person who hasn't met Jesus yet? Think of him or her as a soul who needs to be loved rather than a sinner who needs to be sorry.

We reach out not only to the lost who've not yet found their way home but also to believers who've drifted off to the far country and are desperate to return. "My brothers and sisters, if one of you should wander from the truth and someone should bring that person back, remember this: Whoever turns a sinner from the error of their way will save them from death and cover over a multitude of sins."[5]

Changed hearts, changed minds, and changed behaviors are

indicators of God at work. "I will give you a new heart and put a new spirit in you; I will remove from you your heart of stone and give you a heart of flesh."[6] Proof of new life isn't people praising you or your beautiful fruit. It's people praising God and telling others about Him.

Heavenly Father,
I know that any fruit in my life
comes from Your gardening efforts
and not my own.
Thank You for tending me
with such loving care
so I can keep growing,
keep blooming, and keep bearing fruit
that is pleasing to You.

One Minute, One Step

**Nourishment for you,
nourishment for others.**

Grab a piece of fresh fruit. An orange, an apple, a banana, a bunch of grapes—whatever you have on your kitchen counter or in the fridge. No fruit handy? Take sips of coffee or nosh on a protein bar. With each bite or sip pray in earnest for a woman you know who doesn't yet have a relationship with God. Then ask Him how He might use you to plant the seeds of His love in her heart.

*The fruit of the righteous is a tree of life,
and the one who is wise saves lives.*

PROVERBS 11:30

9

Fool's Gold

The way of fools seems right to them,
but the wise listen to advice.

PROVERBS 12:15

*I*f you love to goof around, act silly, or make people laugh—no worries. That's not the kind of foolishness this verse is talking about. God wants to lead us away from egotism and pride and toward humility and a teachable spirit.

The way of fools . . . *Proverbs 12:15*

Foolish people "suppose their way is straight" (CJB) when it's clearly crooked. They "follow their own directions" (VOICE) rather than trusting God's leading. The Lord describes those of us who've been foolish as "headstrong" (MSG) and "stupid" (GNT). It's plural—*fools*—so at least we're not alone, but I'd rather avoid going through life wearing a dunce cap. Not very flattering.

... seems right to them, ... *Proverbs 12:15*

This is the kind of thinking that gets us into trouble. What may sound like wisdom is often foolishness itself. It's the world's wisdom, but it's definitely not God's wisdom. Rather than asking questions, a fool trusts "his own opinion" (NET). He does what is "right in his own eyes" (HCSB) instead of what is truly right. Fools "think they know what is best" (CEV) but end up making things worse.

I know all about such foolishness.

It was 10:16 on a Tuesday night at Detroit Metro Airport. My connecting flight was canceled, the terminal was deserted, and my luggage was nowhere to be seen. I explained my situation to the lone guy at the customer service counter and tried not to whimper when I asked, "How long will it take to retrieve my bag?"

He shrugged. "Could be thirty minutes. Could be two hours. Could be never."

"Never?"

He flipped up his hand, stopping my protest in its tracks. "I'll put in a request, ma'am. But it's only a request, not a promise."

I sank onto a seat facing the empty baggage carousel, discouraged and out of sorts. *Now what?* Everything I needed—fresh clothing, toiletries, makeup, everything—was in that bag. No way could I show up to speak the next day in the Eau-de-Sweat outfit I was wearing that night.

The solution was simple: "Is anyone among you in trouble? Let them pray."[1] If ever there was a perfect time to call on the Lord for help, this was it. Did I make that wise move? Oh, no. I called my husband. It was late at night, and the man was hundreds of miles away. Still, couldn't he do something?

After listening to my moaning and groaning for several minutes, Bill said, "I'm sorry, honey. I'll pray."

"Pray?" I whined. "That's not enough!"

Not enough? Clearly I was exhausted and frustrated and at my wit's end. Caught up in my situation, I'd forgotten what I knew to be true: prayer is the *best* thing we can do and sometimes the *only* thing we can do. Too often I foolishly turn in every direction, looking for answers, instead of turning to the One who has all the answers we'll ever need.

That night in Detroit I sighed in defeat and half-heartedly followed my husband's example. *Please, Lord. I know it's just a suitcase. But if You would send it my way, I'd be grateful.*

The baggage carousel sprang to life. A single bag dropped into view and then slowly began heading in my direction. It was small. It was black. My familiar Mickey Mouse tag dangled from the handle. A here-comes-the-happy-ending soundtrack swelled inside me as I stood, smiling through my tears.

When we put our needs into words, we put our needs into His hands. "Commit your way to the LORD; trust in him and he will do this."[2] God has the power to put the right solution in motion, to calm an anxious heart, to make a crooked path straight. No one cares about your troubles more than the One who loves you most. No one.

. . . but the wise . . . *Proverbs 12:15*

We're ready for a better path, Lord. A way out.

The opposite of a fool is "a sensible person" (CEV). Someone who doesn't do what fools do. They're not stubborn; they're flexible. They're not headstrong; they're cooperative.

What makes them so wise? They open their ears.

. . . listen to advice. *Proverbs 12:15*

One of the qualities people look for in a spouse, an employee, a friend, or a leader is the willingness to listen, to "pay attention" (cjb). We're drawn to those who have ears to hear and use them. And they not only listen; they act. A wise person is "he who heeds" (nkjv). It's beyond frustrating to offer wisdom to someone who's considering doing a foolish thing, only to have that person nod in agreement and then go off and do it anyway.

Wise people know better. They listen, learn, and follow.

When people who know what they are talking about offer useful "counsel" (asv) or "good teaching" (nlv), the wise person says, "Tell me more," even as she prepares herself for news she doesn't want to hear.

Early in my walk with God, I shared with a friend my plan to become the head of women's ministry at our church. We had no such position, but I was convinced that we needed one and that I was the person for the job. My friend heard me out and then said, "Liz, what I'm sensing from you right now is an overflow of pride. A desire to lead but not a desire to serve." Hard as that was to hear, I knew she was right. When the church gently turned down my offer to lead, I was even more certain of her assessment. "Wounds from a friend can be trusted,"[3] especially when that friend knows you well and has a close relationship with the Lord.

One path I've learned to avoid is gathering lots of opinions. Nothing gets us off track faster than listening to what everybody and their sister have to say. If others affirm what we've sensed from the Lord, have read in His Word, and have heard from wise counselors, then all is well and good. But let's steer clear of seeking feedback on social media or among a wide group of acquaintances. Though people "delight in airing their own opinions,"[4] God's opinion is the one that matters.

It can be hard to admit we need direction, to raise our hands, to seek advice. Yet that's what God calls wisdom. The best part? When wise people heed wise counsel, it makes them even wiser. No fooling.

Lord Jesus,
I've opted for foolishness
rather than asked for advice
more times than I can count.
You know them all
and have forgiven them all.
I live in Your debt, Lord.
I'm so grateful You know me
better than I know myself.

One Minute, One Step

Make time for what matters.

Set the alarm on your watch or smartphone for a time you're sure to be available in the next twelve hours. When the alarm goes off, use that reminder to prompt you to pray about a pending decision, and then be still and listen for God's tender voice offering you wise counsel.

The way of fools seems right to them,
but the wise listen to advice.

PROVERBS 12:15

10

Heavy Lifting

Anxiety weighs down the heart,
but a kind word cheers it up.

PROVERBS 12:25

nxiety. It can range from a fleeting sense of worry to a
serious illness that affects millions. For those who suffer from anxiety disorder, the right prescription might restore our
bodies to a healthy chemical balance. For others, the right word at
the right time could be enough to lift our burdens and brighten
our spirits.

Whatever *anxiety* means to you, my friend, this verse offers
good medicine.

Anxiety . . . *Proverbs 12:25*

The cares of life can quickly rob us of joy and drain us of
hope. A feeling of "heaviness" (asv) can settle into our souls,
whether from "grief" (dra) or "sorrow" (ylt) over a recent loss or

an overwhelming sense of "worry" (EXB) about what might happen next.

When we let our imaginations wander down What-If Boulevard, when we visit Worst-Case-Scenario Town one too many times, fear of the future can become an unbearable burden. Instead, let's give our fears to God and tell the Enemy to take a hike.

Fear is one of the Adversary's favorite ways to distract and discourage. It often comes double wrapped in guilt and shame so that we're afraid to take even a tiny step of faith, let alone a leap. Soon we feel as if the whole world is resting on our shoulders, when the truth is, it rests on His.

. . . weighs down the heart, . . . *Proverbs 12:25*

Imagine an unseen emotion pressing down on us until we "stoop" (ASV) and are brought "low" (DRA). Like "a heavy load" (NCV) that "drags us down" (VOICE), anxiety not only affects us on the inside; it can also change us on the outside. Our shoulders droop, our eyes are downcast, and people start asking, "Are you okay?"

This is the hardest part: admitting something's wrong. Confessing "No, I'm not okay" first to ourselves and then to someone we trust. The good news? God already knows about your heart condition. He is even now sending help. One of His children is bringing just what you need.

. . . but a kind word . . . *Proverbs 12:25*

It's amazing what an "encouraging word" (AMPC) can do. Recently I shared with a friend my desperate desire to make a change in my life. With each halting step forward, I texted her an update. Each time she texted back a "good word" (CEB):

"I am so very, very proud of you."

"Keep going."

"You've made my day!!!"

"I am believing God, my friend."

"Come on!!!"

If you need to hear those words, beloved, take them. They are meant for you too. So are these: "Be strong and courageous. Do not be afraid or terrified because of them, for the LORD your God goes with you; he will never leave you nor forsake you."[1]

Never leave you. Never forsake you. Now, those are some *really* good words.

. . . cheers it up. *Proverbs 12:25*

The end result of a kind word from a friend? Or, even better, from God's Word? Our eyes brighten. Our spirits lift. Possibilities begin to surface. Hope rises in our hearts. A good word makes us "glad" (ASV). It brings us "joy" (NET) and "lightens our day" (VOICE). The truth is, "a word of encouragement does wonders!" (TLB).

As delightful as it is to receive such words, it's even more fun to share them. An uplifting comment is the least expensive, most effective gift we can give others. Just two words—"Nice dress!" or "Great job!"—can make a difference.

When we're alone, we may need to cheer ourselves up. Driving by myself to a local speaking engagement where I would be sharing a new message, I poured out all my concerns to God. (Yes, aloud. In the car. It's okay if no one else is with you, right?) "Help, Lord. I'm afraid I don't have enough material. Or too much material. I'm afraid that it's too heavy for a Friday night. Or that the opening story won't work. Or . . ."

God quickly put a stop to my anxious fretting by bringing to my mind the words of His Son: "Do not let your hearts be troubled and do not be afraid."[2]

I changed my tune at once. "I am *not* afraid. I am excited!" In fact, I was *so* eager I had to make myself stay below the speed limit, and when I got there, I practically ran across the parking lot. Only God can banish our anxious thoughts that quickly. As the psalmist wrote, "When anxiety was great within me, your consolation brought me joy."[3]

Heavenly Father,
kind words are often
in short supply.
Let me be thankful
when I receive them
and generous about
giving them to others.
Words matter, Lord.
Your Word most of all.

One Minute, One Step

Take a deep breath, and then
speak a kind word.

Step outside for a moment or simply stand where you are. Slowly breathe in, filling your lungs. Hold the air inside you for a moment, and then gradually exhale, releasing your anxious thoughts to the One who loves you. When was the last time you paused long enough to do that?

Next, plan to say a kind word to the next person you see. Not expecting to bump into anyone today? Say a kind word to yourself. Right now.

Anxiety weighs down the heart,
but a kind word cheers it up.

PROVERBS 12:25

II

Tongue-Tied

Those who guard their lips preserve their lives,
but those who speak rashly will come to ruin.

PROVERBS 13:3

few times (very few) I wish I'd spoken up instead of holding back. But many times (way too many) I wish I'd held my tongue. At home. At work. On a plane. In a restaurant. At church. At a friend's house . . . Well, pretty much everywhere.

Though apologies can be made, and humble pie can be served for dinner, words spoken can't be unspoken. We may try to explain or beg to be forgiven, but we can't undo the damage we've already done.

Those who guard their lips . . . *Proverbs 13:3*

World War II posters reminded Americans "Loose lips might sink ships." It's still wise counsel today. "People who are careful about what they say" (ERV) not only protect themselves; they also guard the safety and well-being of others.

In the book of Proverbs, more than a hundred verses teach us about the power of our words to wound or to heal: "The words of the reckless pierce like swords"—*oof!*—"but the tongue of the wise brings healing."[1]

Planting this truth in my head and heart isn't enough. I need to educate my mouth as well: "Self-control means controlling the tongue!" (TLB). Right. I not only respond too quickly; sometimes I speak while the other person is still talking. Good grief.

Recently I was chatting with a younger woman who lost her train of thought for a moment. She confessed, "Sometimes my brain works faster than my mouth."

"That's okay," I told her. "At my age my mouth works faster than my brain."

Short of taping our lips shut, what can we do to control our tongues when we're around people? **Stop. Look. Listen. Pray.**

We can **stop** thinking about how we might answer and **look** at the other person's eyes, expression, and body language. We can **listen** to what he or she is saying and **pray** before we offer a response.

When in doubt, it's usually best to say nothing. If you "keep what you know to yourself" (CEV), you'll stop hearsay in its tracks, remain a trustworthy friend, and save yourself and others a ton of trouble. At times I have to literally press my lips together—hard—as I pray for the Lord to rescue me from a possible disaster.

. . . preserve their lives, . . . Proverbs 13:3

This is God's saving power at work. Because of His mercy and loving-kindness, the Holy Spirit helps us before we end up in deep water and drag others down with us. Calling on Him first to zip our lips is far more effective than crying out to Him after we're drowning in a sea of poorly chosen words.

Our verse from Proverbs promises that if you control your mouth, "you will be safe" (CEV). Whether you picture a life preserver tossed in your direction or a safety net stretched below you or a fire escape outside your window, guarding your speech ensures you will "take another breath" (VOICE).

Such a good plan.

Now let's look at the second half of this verse, the cautionary part, the warning that comes after *but.*

. . . but those who speak rashly . . .
Proverbs 13:3

You'd think the assurance of safety would be enough to keep believers in line. But for some of us, "Careful words make for a careful life" (MSG) isn't our motto. Instead of holding back our thoughts, words, or opinions, we let them rip, telling ourselves we're just being honest, just telling it like it is.

The original Hebrew, translated here as "speak rashly," means "open wide." This is a "careless talker" (GNT), the kind of person who speaks "without thinking" (NIrv) and "talks too much" (ISV).

Those who "open their lips" (CEB) often have a hard time closing them. With "no guard on his speech" (DRA), a person is likely to say anything. When we're frustrated, we blurt out words we wouldn't normally say. And when we're angry, we shout out words we wouldn't even allow ourselves to *think* if we were feeling calm and behaving rationally.

Then what happens to us and the people we care about?

. . . will come to ruin. Proverbs 13:3

Families destroyed. Jobs lost. Marriages ended. Bank accounts emptied. Relationships severed. This isn't my inner drama queen talking. The Hebrew word translated "ruin" literally means "terror." The rash words we speak can do frightening damage.

I'll bet you can think of a time when a sharp rebuke or blast of vitriol became a weapon of mass "destruction" (ASV) in a friendship, in a household, in a workplace. The minute the words explode from our mouths, we have the sickening realization we're "done for" (CEV). It's seldom a calculated attack meant to inflict injury. It's more often a thoughtless remark, "a quick retort" (TLB), nothing more than "careless talk" (MSG), yet it could "ruin everything" (NLT).

Okay, now I'm nervous. Maybe we should resist the urge to say anything. Keep our mouths permanently shut. But that's not God's will for us. He urges us to "teach and admonish one another with all wisdom,"[2] and to "speak as those approved by God."[3]

Speaking isn't the problem; it's controlling our wild and willful tongues. That's where we need the Holy Spirit's help. He alone can intercede, guard our thoughts, stop our words, and keep us from sinning. Jesus told His followers, "But when he, the Spirit of truth, comes, he will guide you into all the truth."[4] If we heed His guidance, we can trust Him to keep our words in check.

(Ever feel like a verse in the Bible was written just for you? Whew.)

Heavenly Father,
before I open my mouth,
help me choose my words with care.
Guard them with Your Spirit.
Temper them with Your love.
Fill them with Your grace.
Remind me that
wrong words lead to disaster
but right words can lead
to everlasting life.

One Minute, One Step

Picture this solution.

Silently counting to ten might keep you from exploding, but then it's hard to listen to the other person or to the Lord. Here's another plan. Draw a picture of your mouth— with or without lipstick. Now add a simple lock and key in the center. The next time you feel a head of steam building, call this picture to mind and imagine yourself turning the key and then slipping it into your pocket. Trust me on this one. It's surprisingly effective.

Those who guard their lips preserve their lives,
but those who speak rashly will come to ruin.

PROVERBS 13:3

12

Home Deconstruction

The wise woman builds her house,
but with her own hands the foolish one tears hers down.

PROVERBS 14:1

When a group of married girlfriends gathered with me to study Proverbs 31 one summer, I gave them a homework assignment: "Ask your husband, 'What speaks love to you?'"

You might be surprised at their answers. We certainly were.

One husband said he treasured the look in his wife's eyes when he entered the room. Another said the way his wife addressed him in conversation revealed her true feelings for him. And a third husband confessed that the sacrifices his wife willingly made on their behalf were the deepest expression of her love for him.

Just. Wow.

Clearly, these men were grateful for wives who lived out God's Word in their homes.

The wise woman . . .
Proverbs 14:1

Being wise means so much more than being intelligent or educated or talented or clever. Wisdom comes from knowing God. It's a female noun in Hebrew, *chokmoth,* paired here with *ishshah,* meaning "woman, wife, female." And it's plural. God applauds not just one wise woman but "every wise woman" (AMPC). In truth, "the wisest of women" (ESV).

That can definitely be you.

. . . builds her house, . . .
Proverbs 14:1

Rather than a house of boards and concrete and roofing shingles, this is a home built with our hearts and minds, through God's Spirit and God's truth. In the original Hebrew the word translated "house" means "household." Rather than our physical residences, it's everyone who gathers beneath our roofs and finds sanctuary there.

A wise and godly woman "strengthens her family" (NCV) and "makes her home what it should be" (ERV). Not a *House Beautiful* mansion or a Pinterest-ready showplace, but a grace-filled, love-centered, bursting-with-joy, covered-with-peace, don't-mind-the-dust, kick-off-your-shoes kind of home. And if you live by yourself in an apartment no bigger than a walk-in closet? It's still home—your home—where people can be welcomed and God can be honored.

When I embraced the grace of God in my late twenties, I was a single woman with my own little urban fixer-upper. One of the first things I did was hang a huge portrait of Jesus in my entrance hall. A bit much? Maybe. But interior design wasn't the point. I wanted the Lord front and center in my life. I needed His loving expression to greet me when I walked in the door and His gentle gaze to send me off to work.

I also needed His Word posted on my fridge, on my mirror, and on my walls to remind me of His grace and to help remake me in His image. I knew the darkness I'd come from, and I didn't want to go back.

> . . . but with her own hands . . .
> *Proverbs 14:1*

Uh-oh. Here the word *but* prepares us for the rest of the story about a not-so-wise woman.

This emphasis on "her own actions" (ERV) means the girl can't blame anybody else. She made a mess of things "by her own efforts" (TLB) and did so not with good intentions but "with her own evil works" (WYC).

We've seen this. Some of us have done this. We had happiness in our grasp and then threw it away, even as people around us whispered, "Fool!"

> . . . the foolish one tears hers down. *Proverbs 14:1*

Calling such a woman "unwise" (WYC) may soften the blow, but it's worth considering that the Hebrew word for "foolish" comes from the same root as the word for "evil." A foolish woman isn't merely careless or thoughtless or hormonal. She's traveling downward and dragging her household with her.

The woman who turns away from God and His wisdom eventually turns her beautiful home into an abandoned ruin. If you've lived long enough, you've seen this happen—to a family member, a coworker, a friend. Heartbreaking.

It's hard to watch when "the home of a foolish woman is destroyed" (ERV). We can shout out warnings, jump up and down, and wave our arms, but without God's goodness to keep her from sinning, "brick by brick" (MSG) she "plucks it down" (JUB) and "picks it to splinters" (VOICE).

Of all the cautionary, don't-go-there verses in the Bible, this one hits especially hard because it's directed at us, sisters. We have the power to build up our loved ones, and we also have the means to tear them down.

I can't bear to end on such a grim note, so let's circle back to the hopeful start. "Homes are made by the wisdom of women" (GNT). If we throw ourselves on God's mercy, if we give Him the keys to our dwelling places, if we seek His wisdom and ignore the voice of the Adversary, then we can say with confidence, "The rain came down, the streams rose, and the winds blew and beat against that house; yet it did not fall, because it had its foundation on the rock."[1]

Lord Jesus,
I love happy endings,
not because they pacify me,
but because they glorify You.
In my home, in my family,
in my circles of influence,
help me seek to be a wise woman,
caring for those around me,
building up instead of tearing down,
serving others rather than serving myself.

One Minute, One Step

Shore up your household physically and spiritually.

Looking ahead to your next meal at home, choose an encouraging word—*peace, joy, love, hope*—and spell it out on a plate as a centerpiece, using macaroni, raisins, cereal, dried beans, or whatever's handy. Cover it with plastic wrap if you have pets or young children at home.

Later, when you gather around the table, ask your family or friends what aspects of your home reflect this encouraging word. Dining alone? Answer the question yourself. You deserve a peaceful, joyful, loving, hope-filled home too.

The wise woman builds her house,
but with her own hands the foolish one tears hers down.

PROVERBS 14:1

13

Less Is Best

Better a little with the fear of the LORD
than great wealth with turmoil.

PROVERBS 15:16

What do you want more of in your life? And what do you want less of? If we wrote it all down, we'd probably go through a ream of paper. This proverb captures it in fourteen words. The Lizzie Revised Version (LRV) whittles it down to three: *less is best.*

Better a little . . . *Proverbs 15:16*

Sadly, it's "better to live with less" (VOICE) is not what our culture teaches us. In fact, "better to have little" (NLT) is the very opposite of what comes blaring out of our television sets or scrolling across our computer screens. Instead we hear "Life is better with more. More money to buy more things to look more attractive to have more status to gain more attention to make more money to buy more things . . ."

This cycle isn't just vicious. It's deadly. It's everything the Lord doesn't want for us. He knows that riches, possessions, good looks, privilege, and fame are fleeting at best and worthless in light of eternity. That's why He urges us to lead "a simple life" (MSG), free from striving after more, more, more. He assures us "it is better to be poor" (ERV) than to choke on the riches of this world.

Confession? The words I'm writing and the life I'm living aren't entirely in sync. See, I love *more.* My home, my body, and my calendar are living proof. Even as my fingers move across the keyboard, God is pressing on my heart. His words are loving, but they are not subtle. *It's not enough for you to read My Word, Liz. When are you going to live My Word?*

I desperately want to say, "Now, God." But what comes out is, "*How,* God? How do I—how do all of us—stop wanting more?"

His answer is swift and sure: "how wide and long and high and deep is the love of Christ."[1] That's *more,* all right. It covers everything.

His love is more than enough.

His grace is more than sufficient.

His mercy is more than we deserve.

His power is more than we can imagine.

His loving-kindness is what makes *how* possible. God has something finer for us, far more than we can fathom. Our *little* becomes *much* when we see Him high and lifted up and fall to our knees.

. . . with the fear of the LORD . . . *Proverbs 15:16*

When we're scared, we run, we hide, we look the other way. That's not what God wants. He wants us to run toward Him, to fix our eyes on Him, to be overwhelmed by His beauty. To whisper in amazement, "Who is like you—majestic in holiness, awesome in glory, working wonders?"[2] To worship Him with our lives and honor Him with our obedience.

When we experience a "reverent, worshipful fear of the Lord" (AMPC), when we "respect" (ERV) and "honor the Eternal" (VOICE), it's easier to sort out our selfish wants from our genuine needs. To distinguish our shallow *more* from His wise *less*.

As the writer of Hebrews declares, "Let us be thankful, and so worship God acceptably with reverence and awe."[3] He is more than worthy of our praise and adoration. God deserves to be first. Above things. Above people. Above all.

. . . than great wealth . . . *Proverbs 15:16*

Is money on your "What I want more of" list? God understands. We need a certain amount of cash just to feed, clothe, and shelter ourselves and those we love. Excessive wealth is what He's cautioning us about—living "a rich life" (MSG) and counting on our "treasure" (AMP) to make us happy. The Lord knows better. We know better.

The same televisions that urge us to buy more, more, more also show us news stories of the rich and famous who are utterly miserable. Wealth can solve a few day-to-day problems, but it's a poor salve for heartache or disappointment.

The writer of Ecclesiastes puts it perfectly: "Yet when I surveyed all that my hands had done and what I had toiled to achieve, everything was meaningless, a chasing after the wind; nothing was gained under the sun."[4] Yes, we've seen this. The inheritance money that turned siblings into enemies. The full bank account that couldn't make up for an empty life. The new job with higher pay that ended up costing far too much.

. . . with turmoil. *Proverbs 15:16*

Whether you call it "inner turmoil" (NLT) or "tumult" (YLT) or just plain "trouble" (ASV), no one wants it. A big house, a fine car, and a closet full of designer clothes are no prize when they're "coupled with worry" (CJB) and produce "a ton of headaches" (MSG).

We usually think we'll be the exception. We tell ourselves, "Should a fortune come my way, I'd know how to spend it wisely." Then, if the money appears, our best intentions are left in tatters.

Help, Lord.

He *is* helping, right here in this verse. He's giving us a heads-up, sparing us from discovering that when we chase after riches, we have to "carry the burdens that come with them" (VOICE). He's showing us the truth: "It's better to obey the LORD and have only a little, than to be very rich and terribly confused" (CEV).

Who needs more confusion? Just give me Jesus.

Lord, I'm listening.
Truly, I am.
I've chased after
all the wrong things long enough.
I know what it means to feel empty.
I'd rather be filled with You.

One Minute, One Step

Count your blessings.

Empty your wallet or one of the pockets in your purse, and then get rid of all the bits of lint, the dog-eared receipts, the gum wrappers, the ticket stubs. Once your wallet or purse pocket is clean and dusted, count the cash, the loose change, the credit cards. Whatever the amount, whatever your credit limit, thank God for His provision.

When you put everything back in place, you'll find your wallet or purse is not only thinner—it's also lighter and easier to carry.

Better a little with the fear of the LORD
than great wealth with turmoil.

PROVERBS 15:16

14

How We Roll

*Commit to the LORD whatever you do,
and he will establish your plans.*

PROVERBS 16:3

The old saying "If you want to hear God laugh, show Him your plans" surely must be true, because I've heard His holy laughter rolling down from heaven many times in my life.

Some of us have a five-year plan and a ten-year plan, plus goals for each year, each month, each week, each day, each hour, each minute. Others take life one day at a time with a few scribbled notations on next week's calendar. And even if we don't write things down, we often carry our plans in our hearts. *Next week I'm starting this. Next month I plan to tackle that. Next year I'm getting my act together. Finally.*

We've got it all figured out. We are working our plan.

Nothing wrong with that as long as we understand we'll be

following a path already laid out for us by the One who knows every step we're going to take in life, from beginning to glorious end. "In their hearts humans plan their course, but the LORD establishes their steps."[1]

You can be sure God's plan for you is the very best plan.

> Commit to the LORD whatever you do, . . .
> *Proverbs 16:3*

Now get ready for a big, juicy *aha*. The words "commit," "trust" (NLV), and "depend" (EXB) are fine translations, but the original Hebrew word gives us a wonderful word picture. *Galal* means "to roll." To physically push something away from you. To release it. To let it roll away.

Imagine pushing your daily "activities" (HCSB) off your shoulders and onto His. Releasing the burdens that crush your spirit. Rolling your long to-do list into His able hands and then letting Him put things in order and check off each item for you. *Done.*

That's what this verse from Proverbs asks us to do. "Roll your works upon the Lord" (AMPC). First we trust Him to guide us from one task to the next, according to His will. Then we put our faith in His choices and let go of the need to control every minute. Finally we stop measuring a productive day by what we have accomplished, and instead we celebrate what God has accomplished in and through us.

> . . . and he will establish your plans.
> *Proverbs 16:3*

God leaves nothing to chance or whim. What we call inter-ruptions, He calls perfect timing. What we consider mistakes, He considers lessons. Because of His boundless love, your "thoughts shall be directed" (DRA) by Him, and "He will cause your thoughts to become agreeable to His will" (AMPC).

Wait. Is this like brainwashing? Not at all. It's His sovereignty in action as you "fix your thoughts on Jesus, whom we acknowl-edge as our apostle and high priest."[2] God promises us that the plans we turn over to Him "will work out well" (NLV), because He is alive and well and at work in us.

In those moments when I can't imagine how God will ever clean up the latest mess I've made, I turn to this verse and hang on with trembling hands: "For nothing will be impossible with God."[3] *Nothing* means not one thing is too big for God, too hard for God, too much for God. And if nothing is *impossible,* that means everything must be *possible* with God. That's right. "God can do anything!"[4] Astonishing, isn't it? Now watch this.

Four of the most powerful words ever spoken—"God can do anything"—can be reduced to three words without losing an ounce of energy. "God can do." Even two words. "God can." Yes, even one word. "God."

Consider what He did one wintry Saturday morning in Chicago.

Hundreds of women had gathered for an annual Christmas brunch. Decorations sparkled, lights twinkled. Once the hotel staff began clearing the tables, I felt that familiar tightening in my stomach. Almost time to speak. Definitely time to pray.

Standing backstage, I bowed my head. *Lord, I want to be invisible. Make this day all about You and Your Word and not at all about Lizzie and my words. Let them see only You on this platform.* I realize it's tricky *not* to be seen on a brightly lit stage, but I knew that's what God had prompted me to pray, so I went with it.

Once I was introduced, I tossed out a little humor to help us all relax and then began sharing the story of Mary of Nazareth, focusing on the angel Gabriel's miraculous promise to her: "For with God nothing shall be impossible."[5] Even though I was speaking straight from the heart, putting my whole self into the message, something wasn't working. I felt no real connection with the audience. Yes, I was speaking, and they were kindly listening. But nothing was happening.

Then God came to my rescue. The lights on the stage blinked out so quickly the audience gasped. I could still see the women, but they couldn't see me. At all.

"Lord, I want to be invisible." God had answered my prayer— well, His prayer—though not in the way I'd expected. While people backstage scrambled to find a solution, I knew God had already taken care of everything.

I was in the dark so He could shine.

Standing center stage, I explained to the audience the words of my prayer and God's miraculous answer. "Truly, God can do anything!" Then, trusting Him to give me all the words they needed to hear, I abandoned my notes, moved closer to the audience, and shared His message instead of mine.

Do I remember what I said? Not a word. I remember only the sheer *power* of His presence in that room. We all sensed it, knowing this shared experience had nothing to do with me and everything to do with God—precisely as He'd planned.

Heavenly Father,
help me lay down my plans
and trust Your plans instead.
You really can do anything
and surely will do everything
according to Your will.

One Minute, One Step

※

**Since God can do anything,
let's see what He can do in your life.**

Write down one much-needed change that seems impossible to achieve, whether it's losing weight, keeping your house tidy, getting up early every day to study God's Word, or making regular deposits to a savings account. Something big, something hard, something you've tried to do before and failed.

Are you ready to roll that challenge onto the Lord's shoulders? To stop trying and start trusting? To believe not that you can do it but that He can do it?

*Commit to the LORD whatever you do,
and he will establish your plans.*

PROVERBS 16:3

15

Worth the Wait

Hope deferred makes the heart sick,
but a longing fulfilled is a tree of life.

PROVERBS 13:12

When someone says, "I have good news and bad news," which one do you want to hear first? I usually vote for the bad news, thinking it's better to get it over with and end on a happier note. You could also make a solid case for starting with the good news so you can have a positive mind-set for whatever follows.

In this proverb the hard truth comes first.

Hope deferred . . . *Proverbs 13:12*

It's been a difficult season for many people you and I know. Hope is in short supply when job hunts lead nowhere and health challenges aren't improving and family issues won't go away. Our

Lord Jesus understands what "unrelenting disappointment" (MSG) feels like. He knows that "not getting what you want" (CEV) is frustrating and discouraging. He realizes that when hope is "postponed" (VOICE), "prolonged" (YLT), or "put off" (NIrV), we need something to hang on to.

Something bigger than hope.

Something deeper than desire.

Something immovable. Something sure.

That's why the Lord wants us to hang on to Him. He's waiting for the moment we come to the end of ourselves, our plans, our dreams and at last begin to realize that our hope is found only in Him. "I wait for the LORD, my whole being waits, and in his word I put my hope."[1] *Yes.*

We can put our hope in God's spoken, written, printed Word and all the wisdom, promises, and truth it contains. We can put our hope in God's character and the ways He reveals it through what He has already said and what He has already done. We can put our hope in God's Son, His living Word.

A friend clung to this verse from Proverbs while waiting for an adoption to be finalized, a process that took *four long years.* Not weeks. Not months. *Years.* Yet she knew she wasn't waiting alone. God was with her, and His Word was with her. This proverb in particular sustained her during the shadowy days and strengthened her when nothing seemed certain.

Even with God beside us, waiting can still be hard.

. . . makes the heart sick, . . . *Proverbs 13:12*

"When hope is crushed, the heart is crushed" (GNT), so much so it not only "makes you sad" (ERV), but it can also "make you feel sick" (CEV). We moan inwardly or cry outwardly as the psalmist did: "Why, my soul, are you downcast? Why so disturbed within me?"[2] Disappointment "grieves the heart" (VOICE) and "tormenteth the soul" (WYC). Those who've experienced that level of emotional and spiritual pain know how the body often suffers too. Head throbbing. Stomach twisting. Muscles aching.

Heartsickness is real. So is the remedy, as the psalmist concludes: "Put your hope in God, for I will yet praise him, my Savior and my God."[3] *Yet* means it's never too late to praise Him. This very minute our praise can begin to rise from our lips and ascend to the heavens. Praise Him in the midst of the heartache, the psalmist urges us. When hope is waning, trust Him as your one true Source of hope.

. . . but a longing fulfilled . . . Proverbs 13:12

Call it a "wish" (CEV), a "dream" (NLT), or a "desire" (ASV), but when it "comes into being" (NLV), gladness floods our soul and healing fills our bones. *How did I ever doubt?* we ask ourselves, unable to keep from smiling and shaking our heads in wonder.

We doubt because we are human. We believe because He is divine.

To move from doubt to belief requires a leap of faith, which often looks less like leaping and more like waiting, praying, and trusting, as these verses from Psalms teach us:

"Wait for the LORD; be strong and take heart and wait for the LORD."[4]

"Hear my prayer, LORD; let my cry for help come to you."[5]

"LORD Almighty, blessed is the one who trusts in you."[6]

Oh, the fruit of that waiting, praying, and trusting!

. . . is a tree of life. *Proverbs 13:12*

When we hang on to hope and don't lose heart, God will produce in us a whole tree bearing vital food for our souls. Hope grows in a heart made fertile by God's Word, refreshed by His living water, and warmed by the light of His love every season of the year. As Pope Francis said in his 2017 TED Talk, "Hope is a humble, hidden seed of life that, with time, will develop into a large tree."[7]

When our prayers are answered and our needs are met, it's "like eating fruit from the tree of life" (NCV). All at once "life is full and sweet" (VOICE), and we find ourselves back on our feet. The Hebrew phrase for this "tree of life" is the same one we find in Genesis 2:9 describing a unique tree in the middle of Eden's garden. Here in Proverbs the meaning expands to include a full life—mental and emotional, moral and spiritual—that lasts forever.

Heartache is a certainty in life. But so, dear friend, is God, the Source of our hope.

Lord Jesus,
I lose heart and lose hope regularly.
I worry on my own instead of waiting with You.
I forget that it's best to pray sooner rather than later.
I let my trust turn to rust
and my hope turn to dust.
And then, Lord, You bring them back.
You restore my hope
in You.

One Minute, One Step

Go on a search for hope.

Turn to the concordance or index in the back of your Bible. Or use your computer or smartphone to open Bible Gateway.com or your favorite online Bible. Now look up the word *hope* in Romans. *Hope* appears there more than in any other book of the New Testament. Write down one verse that gives you an extra measure of hope for today.

Hope deferred makes the heart sick,
but a longing fulfilled is a tree of life.

PROVERBS 13:12

16

Soul Food

Gracious words are a honeycomb,
sweet to the soul and healing to the bones.

PROVERBS 16:24

Sweet. Delicious. Mouthwatering. And no calories. Not a one. This tasty verse from Proverbs is a divine recipe for good health. Reach for a spoon.

Gracious words . . . *Proverbs 16:24*

What if the only words we spoke to one another were "pleasant" (LEB) and "kind" (CEV) and "fair" (GNV)? How would it change things if we filled the air with "gracious speech" (MSG), with carefully chosen and "well ordered" (DRA) words, with nothing spoken out of anger or pain or frustration or guilt? And what if we used our words to "encourage one another and build each other up"[1] rather than discourage and tear each other down?

You know the answer. The world would be forever changed. The Enemy of our souls would be completely undone. No wonder so many of us love this verse!

"Delightfulness, favor, beauty." That's the whole of what the Hebrew word, here translated as "gracious," means. Imagine if we began each day with this simple prayer request: "Let the beauty of the LORD our God be upon us."[2] Yes, and especially upon our words.

There is a brief moment, a mere nanosecond, between when we open our mouths and words pour out. What if we took the faintest breath, the slightest pause, and gave that window of time to God so the Holy Spirit could serve up something sweet to the ear?

. . . are a honeycomb, . . . *Proverbs 16:24*

Few verses are as flavorful as this one. You can almost taste the "flowing honey" (CEB), catch the fragrant aroma of "clover" (MSG), feel the smooth "liquid" (EXB) on your tongue. Picture stirring a spoonful of golden honey into a cup of hot tea, skimming a knife laden with honey across warm, buttered toast, or drizzling a dollop of honey over steaming porridge. *Mmm.*

Are you hungry yet? Perhaps that's God's intent with this verse from Proverbs. To whet our appetite for His Word. To make us eager to taste, chew, swallow, and digest the banquet He has prepared for us. David described God's commands as "sweeter than honey."[3] And when God told Ezekiel to consume a scroll covered with His words, the prophet confessed, "I ate it, and it tasted as sweet as honey in my mouth."[4]

When we feast on God's Word, our words will echo His. And when we put Him at the center of our relationships, they are all the sweeter for it.

Bill and I were somewhere in the rolling hills of Virginia, enjoying our third night together as newlyweds. He was taking a shower, and I was channel surfing. By the time my handsome husband reappeared, freshly shaved and wrapped in a towel, I was deeply engrossed in a Billy Graham sermon on television.

Bill joined me at the end of the bed. "Not exactly how I pictured spending our honeymoon," he teased. Minutes later he was watching the screen as intently as I was. Soon we started discussing effective ways to share the gospel and ended up praying about how we might serve the Lord together in the months and years to come.

That scene set the tone for our whole married life. Hardly a day goes by without some spontaneous exchange of spiritual ideas and beliefs or a lively discussion about Scripture. Scheduling daily devotions together just isn't our thing (sorry!). But regular, meaningful conversations about God and His Word? Absolutely.

Feel free to roll your eyes at this point. It does sound a little too good to be true. We also have days when our words are less than kind and our attitudes less than God honoring. A few doors have been slammed over the years, and more than once we've escaped to opposite ends of the house to keep from saying things we'd regret. Yet through it all, God remains at the heart of our home. His Word and His love make every year better than the one before it.

... sweet to the soul ... *Proverbs 16:24*

Yes, and "sweet to the mind" (AMPC) as well. Such words are "easy to accept" (ERV) and always "delightful" (AMP) since sweetness is the opposite of bitterness.

Kind words can take on a life of their own, affecting others within earshot. On a holiday shopping trip, Lilly and I were standing in a checkout line, chatting about this and that, nothing special. Then I noticed the young cashier had tears in her eyes.

I leaned over and whispered, "Is everything okay?"

Not quite meeting my gaze, she wiped her eyes with her sleeve. "I've just never heard a mother and daughter be that nice to each other."

That was God at work, not Liz and Lilly. When His Word is in our hearts, it's bound to infuse the words we speak to one another. Heaviness gives way to lightness. Discord dissolves into peace. This is why God wants us to dine on His Word. It's good for us—that is to say, it is *good* and it is *for us*. It makes us spiritually healthy, wealthy, and wise.

Wellness doesn't get any better than this.

. . . and healing to the bones. *Proverbs 16:24*

A kind word, especially if it's from His Word, provides "medicine to the bones" (JUB) and "energy for the body" (MSG). When you are feeling weak, God's Word makes you strong. When your joy is waning, God's wisdom is invigorating. Above all, His Word will "bring healing to the body" (NIrV) so you can speak healing words to the people who cross your path.

Even if no one else is listening, He is. Even if no one else cares, He does.

Lord Jesus,
I am grateful
when You speak through me
and am heartbroken
when my own words
get in the way.
Only Your Word can sweeten
a world gone sour.

One Minute, One Step

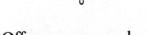

**Offer someone you know
a few gracious words.**

Text, e-mail, or tweet a brief, encouraging word to a friend right now. Make it personal and sincere. Rather than asking a question that requires a response, just let her know you're thinking of her and what you appreciate about her.

*Gracious words are a honeycomb,
sweet to the soul and healing to the bones.*

PROVERBS 16:24

17

Smart Money

How much better to get wisdom than gold,
to get insight rather than silver!

PROVERBS 16:16

*B*ack in the day, entertainer Jack Benny was famous for being frugal. In one comedy skit a thug held him up at gunpoint and demanded, "Your money or your life!" Benny's l-o-n-g pause had the audience in hysterics and prompted the would-be robber to demand again, "I said, 'your money or your life.'" Benny finally confessed, "I'm thinking!"

If we asked the Lord the same question—"Which is worth more: our money or our lives?"—He wouldn't hesitate for a moment. Our hearts, souls, and minds all matter a great deal more than cold, hard cash.

How much better . . .
Proverbs 16:16

We're not talking about a specific number, as in "wisdom is 93 percent more valuable than gold." But increasing our store of wisdom is clearly "worth more" (JUB) than increasing our bank accounts. Wisdom is "preferable" (HCSB) because it's more useful, more shareable, longer lasting, and "more precious" (DRA). Cash is easily spent, never to be reclaimed. Wisdom can be freely given away without losing a single ounce of it.

More good news: Thieves can't break in and steal your wisdom. Nor can you lose it on your next business trip or misplace it in your basement. Whatever wisdom you possess, it's yours to keep forever.

> . . . to get wisdom than gold, . . .
> *Proverbs 16:16*

Gold goes up and down in value, based on the whims of the market. Wisdom only increases. How do we "acquire" (NET) wisdom? How do we "gain" (CJB) or "receive" (VOICE) it? By spending time in God's Word—reading, studying, memorizing—and applying His truth.

A few semesters at the School of Hard Knocks helps too. At least, that's how it works in my life. I learn more when I fail than when I succeed. I learn by stubbornly trying things my way and then contritely doing them God's way. (Nod if any of this sounds familiar.)

In a culture that worships money, those who worship God are called to seek something higher, something finer. As the old hymn says, "I'd rather have Jesus than silver or gold; I'd rather be His than have riches untold."[1] Yes, yes, a thousand times, yes.

... to get insight rather than silver!
Proverbs 16:16

As The Message phrases it, "Choose insight over income every time." Insight is wisdom applied. It's "knowledge" (GNT) and "understanding" (ASV) in action. It's "good judgment" (NLT) and "prudence" (DRA) put to practical, everyday use. Who needs "some silver prize" (VOICE) when we can have the deep satisfaction of pleasing God? "Well done, good and faithful servant!"[2] is worth more than any bonus added to a paycheck.

"But, Liz, we need cash to pay for groceries, utilities, gas." I get that. But this isn't a matter of either/or, of choosing money *or* wisdom. God is merely helping us see which one matters more.

The CEV translates this verse as "It's much better to be wise and sensible than to be rich." As it happens, my wise and sensible husband believes money belongs in the bank. But his carefree and clothes-loving wife thinks money belongs on hangers in her bedroom closet. This has been an ongoing point of ... well, *discussion* in our marriage since the first box from Macy's arrived on our doorstep.

Recently I needed a new raincoat (honest), so I dutifully looked online for the best price I could find in a style I loved. Then I made my pitch. "It's on sale," I explained to Bill, "and shipping is free." Surely *that* would cinch the deal.

"It's not really free," he reminded me. "Shipping is included in the price. Besides, don't you already have a raincoat?" As I said, wise and sensible.

I promised to look in the hall closet before I placed the order, certain I wouldn't find anything. Seriously, who could forget they own a raincoat? The narrow storage area under our staircase is deep and dimly lit, so I almost missed the nice-looking coat hanging way in the back. The one with the tags still attached.

When I pulled it out, I discovered it wasn't just a raincoat. It wasn't just brand-new. It was *the exact same coat* I'd planned to order, purchased two years earlier and never worn because it was too tight. Not only did it fit perfectly now, but it was also my favorite color—red—which the online retailer no longer carried.

I strolled into the family room to show off my find. "I was right," I announced. "The shipping was free!"

"And fast," said my wise and sensible man.

Heavenly Father,
when it comes to gold and silver,
I still have much to learn.
Teach me to value
what You value.
Show me how to wisely invest
in things that last forever.
Help me spend less
so I can give more.

One Minute, One Step

Go shopping in your closet.

Reach deep inside your closet or wardrobe, past the clothes you wear often, to an item you haven't worn in ages (or maybe forgot buying). Try it on. Still fit? Then plan to wear it soon, maybe even today. Not happening? Drop it in a box for your favorite charity shop so another wise and sensible person can go shopping.

How much better to get wisdom than gold,
to get insight rather than silver!

PROVERBS 16:16

18

Good Medicine

A cheerful heart is good medicine,
but a crushed spirit dries up the bones.

PROVERBS 17:22

For years I quoted this verse while watching audiences experience the healing power of laughter. To be honest, I shared only the first half, the cheery part: "A merry heart doeth good like a medicine" (KJV). I've since learned the truth of the second half of the verse and why a "joyful mind" (DRA) is the best remedy in God's medicine cabinet when "a broken spirit drieth the bones" (KJV).

We were in the middle of a difficult holiday season. Bill's father had died of cancer the Saturday before Thanksgiving, so our family gathering was noticeably smaller and definitely sadder. We almost dreaded getting together for Christmas since Mr. Higgs would have turned ninety on December 25. So we saved our celebration for the thirty-first, figuring we'd ring in the New Year by opening presents and sharing happier memories.

Everybody wanted homemade lasagna. My cooking skills are limited, but I can usually manage to layer pasta, ricotta cheese, and tomato sauce in a baking dish without mishap. However, I'd never made two dishes at once—one for the meat lovers and one for the vegetarians in the family. When I reached for some wax paper so I could lay out the freshly cooked pasta to cool, I found to my dismay that the box was empty.

"Just leave the pasta in the hot water," my son suggested. "Maybe add a little oil to keep it from sticking together."

The first dish came together easily enough. But when I started on the second, the slippery, overcooked pasta came out of the water, not in long, ruffled strips, but in oddly shaped hunks. By the time I finished, my veggie lasagna looked like something a five-year-old would make with modeling clay.

Did I burst into tears? I did not. I burst out laughing.

Soon I was laughing so hard I had to sit down. My family, who'd wandered off to admire the Christmas tree, came back into the kitchen. "Mom? Are you all right?"

I was howling by this point, tears streaming down my face. When they saw the lasagna, they understood. Sort of.

All I know is, I hadn't carried on like that in weeks. Months. And this verse from Proverbs is the absolute truth.

A cheerful heart is good medicine, . . . *Proverbs 17:22*

Like an invisible vitamin, cheerfulness "works healing" (AMPC) in your body until at last "you feel good" (CEV). The "curative balm" (VOICE) that happiness provides isn't your imagination working overtime. It's the Lord working full-time. It's the Great Physician providing *gehah*—in Hebrew, "a healing, cure."

The benefits of being joyful are countless. Your blood pressure goes down, your ability to fight infection goes up, and the face you present to the world has fewer frown lines.

Alas, what happens when we lose our joy is another story.

. . . but a crushed spirit . . . Proverbs 17:22

Can you feel the weight of it pressing on your heart? When our spirits are crushed, our eyes give us away. Even if we're smiling, people can see the pain and sadness inside. There's a lack of sparkle, a dullness in our gaze. Despite our best efforts, "sorrow" (ERV) can't be hidden, and a "broken spirit" (ASV) can't be easily mended with a word or two.

"Lighten up!" people tell us. "Snap out of it!" These are not helpful comments for someone with "a downcast spirit" (LEB). For those who feel "gloomy all the time" (GNT), it takes more than a funny story, a humorous cartoon, or a clever one-liner to bring back the joy.

. . . dries up the bones. Proverbs 17:22

In Hebrew *yabesh* means "withered." A perfect description for how genuine depression makes you feel. It's "a disease" (ERV) that "dries you up" (NIrv), that "drains your strength" (EXB) until "you hurt all over" (CEV) and are left "bone-tired" (MSG).

Depression is one of the Enemy's favorite weapons. The debilitation is physical, mental, emotional, biological, spiritual, chemical, and very real.

Is there any hope? Absolutely. If you or someone you love suffers from depression, you are not alone. Your loving Savior can help you take back your life. He may use counselors or physicians or medicines to do so, but you can be sure the healing comes from Him.

A few Aprils ago I was diagnosed with clinical depression. Your ever-joyful Lizzie, who has loved Jesus for more than three decades? Yes. Why mention it here? Because I care about you, dear sister. And if my admission gives you the courage to seek professional help, then praise God.

I will leave any additional advice to those who are qualified to give it, but may I just say there is zero shame in taking an anti-depressant. It's not a crutch for weak people. And it doesn't mean you don't trust God. If your body needs more serotonin, then swallow your pride and swallow the pill your doctor prescribes for you. Please don't let the fear of "What will people think?" keep you from getting the help you need. When our minds and bodies are no longer fighting against us, then joy has a chance to settle into our bones and begin the healing process.

True joy is knowing God and being known by Him. True joy is surrendering to His will and letting Him use any means He chooses to rescue us from darkness and bring us into the light.

He has rescued me. He has rescued many.

Our Jesus, knowing the cross waited for Him, assured His followers, "I have told you this so that my joy may be in you and that your joy may be complete."[1] That's my prayer for you today, beloved: complete joy and freedom in Christ. Even when times are hard, keep a tight grip on this truth: "He will yet fill your mouth with laughter and your lips with shouts of joy."[2]

Lord Jesus,
how I love to laugh.
Thank You for making that possible.
Bless You for calling it holy.
I am ever grateful for
Your good, good medicine.

One Minute, One Step

Look for answers.

Perhaps God has whispered something you needed to hear regarding your lack of joy or a deep sense of discouragement and hopelessness. Here is your task for the next minute. Pray about a person or two you could reach out to: a family member, a friend, a counselor, a minister, a doctor. Someone safe. Write down their names. Find their phone numbers. Ask God for the courage to call one or more of them today.

If depression is not an issue for you, vow to look carefully into the eyes of someone you care about and ask them how they're doing. Then listen with open ears and an open heart.

A cheerful heart is good medicine,
but a crushed spirit dries up the bones.

PROVERBS 17:22

19

Best-Laid Plans

Many are the plans in a person's heart,
but it is the LORD's purpose that prevails.

PROVERBS 19:21

Making plans is a good thing, right? After all, Jesus said, "Suppose one of you wants to build a tower. Won't you first sit down and estimate the cost to see if you have enough money to complete it?"[1] Sounds like planning to me. And when David wrote, "May he give you the desire of your heart and make all your plans succeed,"[2] that suggests we'd need those plans in hand, yes?

Many are the plans . . . *Proverbs 19:21*

Oh, I have sooo many plans. Not merely to-do lists but *must*-do lists, covering the next two years of my life. It's a twenty-seven-page document. I wish I were kidding.

Look, my crazy-busy schedule is nothing to be proud of.

It says, "I can't say no."

It says, "I'm afraid to let go."

It says, "My priorities are out of whack."

It says, "I don't trust anyone else to get the job done."

Whether our lists are written on pale blue lines on paper or appear as tiny pixels on a screen, we keep "brainstorming options" (MSG), coming up with "many devices" (ASV) and creating "all kinds of plans" (EXB).

That's the problem. They're *our* plans. We forget to check with God before we check our calendars. We neglect to seek His counsel before we start looking for something to write on. "We may make a lot of plans" (CEV), but it's worth asking where all those ideas are generated.

. . . in a person's heart, . . . *Proverbs 19:21*

Ah. Human plans, then. Not divine. Some plans that "occupy the mind" (ISV) may reveal questionable motives or selfish desires or outcomes that aren't remotely good for us. We all know "the impulses of the human heart may run wild" (VOICE). When I was twenty, I compiled a bucket list of sorts. Skydiving was near the top. Sometime in my forties I quietly dropped that one. (Jump out of a perfectly good airplane? Not this girl.)

We can make all the plans we like, and we can act as if we have it all together, as if we know what's best for us. But God knows better. Far better.

. . . but it is the LORD's purpose . . .
Proverbs 19:21

Purpose tells us this is not a whim, not a passing notion. God isn't capricious, pushing us around for His amusement. Everything He does is according to His will—His "good, pleasing and perfect will."[3] That's why we can depend on "the counsel of Jehovah" (asv). We can say with the psalmist, "I trust in you, Lord" and "You are my God."[4]

Does His plan always look good and purposeful when we're in the middle of it? Well . . . no, not always. Will it prove to be the best plan when we stand at the finish line? We can count on it. Like the king in his high castle, there is no higher authority than God. He rules. He reigns. His Word is law. His wisdom is final.

We can't predict what our lives will be like even five minutes from now. The phone rings, a letter arrives, a text message appears, and nothing is the same. Yet Jesus is always the same—"yesterday and today and forever."[5] His plan is The Plan.

. . . that prevails. *Proverbs 19:21*

About the only time we hear the word *prevail* anymore is when a weather forecaster talks about prevailing winds. Here *prevail* means "victorious." Literally, the One left standing.

On those days when we lose our bearings and get bogged down in the details of life, knowing this truth can keep us going: God wins. His plan is the ultimate plan, the one that will "succeed" (ceb) and "stand firm" (dra). We can be sure His purpose "wins out in the end" (nirv).

I confess, I love happy endings. Sometimes in movies or books, that final scene can be downright sappy. But in real life? Our forever life? Bring on the hats tossed in the air, the bells ringing, the confetti raining down, the angels singing.

When God wins, "there will be no more death or mourning or crying or pain."[6] When God wins, there will be only joy for His people. You can be sure "the plans of the LORD stand firm forever, the purposes of his heart through all generations."[7] Including our generation. Including this moment.

Heavenly Father,
You know what an obsessive planner I am.
How I believe I'm in charge of my life.
How I think my schedule is my own.
I know better because You know better.
Everything is Yours,
including every hour of every day.
Please, Lord. Please help me let go.

One Minute, One Step

Let God do the planning.

Open your calendar. Delete, cross out, or erase something specific you had planned for later in the day or perhaps later in the week. Free up one full hour at least. Now in the blank space, write *God*. Pray, asking how He wants you to spend this time with Him. No immediate answer? Wait. Resist the urge to fill the hour. Trust Him to use it well.

Many are the plans in a person's heart,
but it is the LORD's purpose that prevails.

PROVERBS 19:21

20

Tower of Power

The name of the LORD is a fortified tower;
the righteous run to it and are safe.

PROVERBS 18:10

If you live in the United States, you've probably seen yellow-and-black signs posted outside schools, fire stations, libraries, and other public buildings with these two words printed on them: Safe Place. Troubled or at-risk youth will find a safe haven there, as well as practical help and people who care.

You and I have a safe place too. A refuge, a sanctuary, where we can run for protection from the Enemy and seek direction from God. The sign we look for? His name. It's a tower stronger than any man-made fortress and large enough to see from a distance, even if we've lost our way.

The name of the LORD . . .
Proverbs 18:10

Christians may call Him "Adonai" (CJB) or "Jehovah" (ASV), even "Yahweh" (HCSB), but our devout Jewish friends are more likely to say "The Shem of Hashem" (OJB). Literally, "The Name of The Name," meant to fill His people with awe.

Religious Jews do not speak or spell out the proper name of God. Rather, YHWH is used, derived from the Hebrew word *havah*, meaning "to be," in past, present, and future tense.[1] The amazing truth wrapped up in His holy name is that God transcends time. He exists then, exists now, and exists forever—simultaneously—a reality our finite human minds can't truly grasp. Perhaps that's why He gives us a powerful image of something we can see and touch, something solid and immovable.

. . . is a fortified tower; . . . Proverbs 18:10

His name is a "strong tower" (ASV), an eternal "fortress" (TLB), a "sturdy watchtower" (VOICE). His name will never fail. His name will never be defeated. His name will never be reduced to rubble. That's why His name instills confidence. It is strong enough, "mighty" (CEV) enough, to provide "a place of protection" (MSG) for those who love Him.

. . . the righteous run to it . . . Proverbs 18:10

We're righteous only because we are "in right standing with God" (AMPC) and are "his people" (CEV). He has chosen us—a truth that continues to astound me every day of my life. We are "the just" (DRA) only because He justifies us. We "do what is right" (ERV) only because His Spirit makes doing the right thing possible. His strong tower of a name is "where the righteous can go" (GNT).

You may be wondering how, exactly, do we run to a name? Here are three ideas to consider.

Speak His name. A shout or a whisper, whatever fits your situation. Do it aloud. Do it expectantly. Just voicing the name of Jesus makes me feel stronger, safer, calmer.

Bill and I were driving through an ice storm several Decembers ago when our car suddenly began to spin out of control on the busy highway. You'd better believe I called out His name! About fifty times, begging for His protection. *Jesus! Jesus! Jesus!* As if in slow motion, we spun through traffic without hitting any other cars and ended up on the broad shoulder of the road without a bruise or a dent. I call that a miracle. And a definite answer to prayer.

Open His Word. In America we have the freedom to buy the Bible, read the Bible, quote the Bible, teach the Bible. His Word is always available to us—on our computers, on our phones, on our nightstands, on our hearts. By running to His Word, we are running into His embrace.

Turn to your favorite book—Psalms, the gospel of John, Romans, Ephesians, 1 John. God will guide you. Now ask Him for whatever you need. Peace? Mercy? Strength? Assurance? Forgiveness? Love? You've come to the right place. "God is our refuge and strength, an ever-present help in trouble."[2]

Seek His church. Since He wants us to "flee to Him" (voice), that could include a house of worship and the people there who serve God. How do you know you've found the right church? If its members welcome you when you're in trouble, afraid, hurting, in need, confused, or on the run, that's the place you want to be.

Jesus said, "It is not the healthy who need a doctor, but the sick."[3] A church is meant to be an infirmary, a hospital, a place where sick people get well. A refuge for the poor, not a resort for the rich. Beautiful to God, rather than merely beautiful to look at. A sanctuary in the truest sense.

. . . and are safe. *Proverbs 18:10*

Safe is definitely good. But the original Hebrew gives us a clearer picture. It means "inaccessibly high." An out-of-reach place where the Enemy cannot touch you—"above danger" (cjb) and "above evil" (amp). What a visual! When you run to the Lord, you are literally "raised up" (jub) and "set safely on high" (net). I'm reminded of my big brother, Tom, carrying me around on his shoulders when I was a toddler. I was high above the floor yet utterly safe in his care as I squealed with delight.

Maybe you're familiar with the contemporary praise song "The Name of the Lord Is a Strong Tower." It's been running through my head while we've been chatting here. This proverb might also remind you of "A Mighty Fortress Is Our God," a hymn written by Martin Luther nearly five centuries ago. Such music stirs our souls, and the lyrics lift our hearts. But The Name of The Name is what keeps us safe.

Heavenly Father,
You are indeed a mighty fortress.
Bless You for holding me up when I feel defeated
and holding me close when I feel forgotten
and keeping me safe when I feel threatened
and keeping me calm when I feel scared.

One Minute, One Step

***

Speak His name. Do it now.

If there are people nearby, whisper. Or simply form with your lips all the names you can think of for God. Here are my favorites from *A* to *Z*. Almighty. Bridegroom. Counselor. Deliverer. Eternal One. Friend. God. Holy One. I AM. Jesus. King of kings. Lord of lords. Master. Name above all names. The One who sees me. Prince of Peace. Quickening Spirit. Redeemer. Savior. Teacher. Upholder. Vine. Wonderful. eXcellent. Yes. Zion's Cornerstone.

The name of the LORD is a fortified tower;
the righteous run to it and are safe.

PROVERBS 18:10

21

In the Spotlight

*The human spirit is the lamp of the LORD
that sheds light on one's inmost being.*

PROVERBS 20:27

For Christmas I bought our outdoorsy son a small but powerful flashlight to slip into his backpack when he goes tramping in the wild. No bigger than his palm, it throws light more than *six hundred feet.* Yet it doesn't come close to the luminous spotlight God shines into the darkest corners of our hearts.

An unsettling thought for most of us. What happens when He finds something embarrassing? Something disgusting? Something we don't want anyone, especially not our holy God, to know about?

Keep reading. The news is good, I promise.

The human spirit . . . *Proverbs 20:27*

Is this the same as the *Holy* Spirit? No, but if you're filled with the Holy Spirit, this is where He dwells inside you. The Hebrew word *neshamah,* translated here as "spirit," means "breath," the very essence of human life. When God formed man from the dust of the ground, He "breathed into his nostrils the breath of life."[1] But it's not oxygen we're talking about. Aardvarks and zebras breathe too. Rather, it's the unique quality that makes us human. Our "conscience" (TLB) or, if you want to get really specific, "that factor in human personality which proceeds immediately from God" (AMPC).

It's the part that makes you *you* and not someone else. The part that's made in God's image, shining inside you.

. . . is the lamp of the LORD . . . *Proverbs 20:27*

Yes, a real lamp, burning bright, like a "fire" (JUB) or a "searchlight" (TLB). This "candle of the LORD" (KJV), Matthew Henry tells us, is "not only lighted by him, but lighted for him"[2] so He can carefully examine the hearts He has created.

. . . that sheds light . . . *Proverbs 20:27*

His beacon inside us "penetrates" (NLT) and "illuminates" (VOICE), relentlessly "searching" (AMP) and "exposing" (NLT) so that the Lord "is able to see" (ERV) everything. I know in my spirit that I can't hide things from God. But in my foolish flesh I tell myself He can't possibly look at all of us at the same time, right? Surely He didn't see me do *that* or hear me mutter *that* or watch me when I behaved like *that*? Yes, He did. And, yes, He can cast His light inside all our hearts at once.

Make no mistake, "the LORD looks deep inside people" (NCV). He sees it all. Why is this a good thing? Because through our God-given conscience, He can show us who we truly are—the good, the bad, and the desperately ugly—so we fully understand we can't possibly manage without Him. As Job wrote, "It is the spirit in a person, the breath of the Almighty, that gives them understanding."[3]

When God sees us, we, too, see ourselves more clearly.

. . . on one's inmost being. *Proverbs 20:27*

Now there's a phrase that would stop a conversation in its tracks: "one's inmost being." Wow. *Heavy,* as we used to say. "Our hearts" (CEV)? We get that. "Our most intimate thoughts" (VOICE)? Sure. "All the hidden things of the bowels" (DRA) sounds like a topic best saved for your next doctor's appointment. And "into your deepest parts" (ERV) makes me downright uncomfortable. It's meant to. In Hebrew the two words for "inmost being"—*cheder* and *beten*—are often translated "bedroom" and "womb." Okay, then.

God shines His light of truth into the very core of who we are—the deepest center of our personality, our sexuality, our physicality, our spirituality—revealing "every hidden motive" (NLT) and "all our innermost secrets" (WYC).

The reality is, "we cannot hide from ourselves" (GNT), and we cannot hide from God. He sees everything, whether we want Him to or not. Yes, that nasty bit. And that. And (sorry) that too. Even so, He loves us. Even so, He forgives us. Even so, He will "cleanse us from all unrighteousness."[4] Because of the sacrifice Christ made on the cross, the penalty for our sins has been paid in full.

When God shines His light inside us, it's not so He can punish us. It's so He can purify us. It's a different kind of light therapy, healing us from the inside out. He brings into the open those shame-filled things we try to conceal so they will no longer chip away at our soul. He cleans out the dark corners where fears linger and brushes away the cobwebs of guilt.

Then comes the best part. The Holy Spirit beams forth, unhindered, as "the light of the righteous shines brightly."[5] Though we can't take credit for the light inside us, we can surely let it shine, let it shine, let it shine.

Lord Jesus,
You know the worst of it.
And You've made the best of it.
I am no longer afraid of Your light,
knowing it reveals
and it heals.
In Your hands, Lord,
it's a beacon of hope.

One Minute, One Step

**Capture the essence of who you
are in a handful of words.**

Now that the light of God's love has shone into your deepest, darkest, truest self, write the opening line of your autobiography, hiding nothing, since God sees everything. Tomorrow you might add another sentence. Begin a journal. Start a book. But for now your opening sentence will be revealing enough.

*The human spirit is the lamp of the LORD
that sheds light on one's inmost being.*

PROVERBS 20:27

22

Looking Glass

*As water reflects the face,
so one's life reflects the heart.*

PROVERBS 27:19

*Y*ou've seen her. That woman who radiates the love of Christ. His truth glows in her eyes. His love shines through her smile. His mercy beams through the words she speaks. Though our society may or may not call her attractive, God calls her beautiful. God calls her His.

Let's take a look in the mirror of His Word and see if that radiant woman might be you. We surely aren't going to look in a full-length mirror to find out if we're beautiful! Not in our one-size-fits-most culture. The pressure to conform—to have the right shape, the right size, the right look—is intense. Yet when God created you, He had a unique plan in mind. A one-size-fits-*you* approach.

I once polled my readers, asking women, "What words come

to mind when you think of your body?" Some responses were predictably negative, but the positive answers were splendid. "Plush, functional, bountiful, dynamic," wrote one woman. "A wonderful piece of machinery," offered another. My favorite body description? "It washes up nicely and never shrinks!" Love it.

God's Word assures us, "He has made everything beautiful in its time."[1] *Everything* would include you and me and all the women we know and admire. The truth is, people take their cue from us. If we're comfortable with who we are, others will be too.

Now that I've joyfully banged my drum on that issue, let's see what wisdom God's Word offers about our viewing our lovely reflection through His eyes.

As water . . . *Proverbs 27:19*

This verse starts with a comparison—"just as" (CJB). In essence Solomon is saying, "Look at how these things are alike and learn." Water can be turbulent, whipped up by the wind. Or it can be calm and placid, like a country lake on a summer morning.

"When you look into water" (NIrV) hoping to catch a clear view of yourself, you need a surface as smooth as glass. Yes, like a mirror.

. . . reflects the face, . . . *Proverbs 27:19*

In ancient days women gazed at their reflections in polished brass.[2] For the poor a simple basin where a woman could see her face "shine in the water" (DRA) often served as a natural "mirror" (NLV). Today clear glass coated with aluminum or silver is the mirror of choice. The reflection you see is only a "likeness" (NIrv), not the real you, though it is your "true face" (VOICE). It's what others see when they look at you.

But that's not what God sees. He looks beyond our mirrored images. He looks inside our hearts and observes the things we do. "For the LORD is a God who knows, and by him deeds are weighed."[3] What deeds of ours might He weigh and find wanting? We won't know the whole story until we stand in His presence. But this is a guarantee: "Now I know in part; then I shall know fully, even as I am fully known."[4]

God sees the absolute truth about who we are and what we've done. Even knowing all that, He loves us completely. As is. As His.

. . . so one's life reflects the heart. *Proverbs 27:19*

In other words, "your thoughts" (CEV), "your heart" (ERV), and "your mind" (NCV) all reveal the real you. The real Susan. The real Donna. The real Lizzie.

What we do and how we live also reflect the state of our hearts. James wrote, "For if you listen to the word and don't obey, it is like glancing at your face in a mirror. You see yourself, walk away, and forget what you look like. But if you look carefully into the perfect law that sets you free, and if you do what it says and don't forget what you heard, then God will bless you for doing it."[5]

It is Christ in us, the hope of glory, that makes us truly beautiful to ourselves, to others, and to God. Our calling is to live and love for Christ. Today. Right now. Not someday when we're ten pounds thinner, but in this body, in this moment, we can "shine like stars in the sky"[6] as we hold out the words of life.

*Lord Jesus, open my eyes so I can be
honest with myself and with others.
Remind me daily that
my appearance is designed by You.
My worth is measured by You.
My calling is bestowed by You.
By the power of the Holy Spirit,
may my life reflect what's in my heart:
You, Lord.
And only You.*

One Minute, One Step

See yourself as God sees you.

Imagine you are standing in front of a full-length mirror. But instead of seeing your reflection, you see the Lord smiling at you with love shining in His eyes. What do you think He sees when He looks at you? What does He see in your mind? And in your heart?

As water reflects the face,
so one's life reflects the heart.

PROVERBS 27:19

23

Do Good

Do not withhold good from those to whom it is due,
when it is in your power to act.

PROVERBS 3:27

*D*uring a recent ice storm, I posted on Facebook a photo of the ice-covered branches outside our window. Among the comments was one from a neighbor: "Liz, do you have power at your house? We don't."

My heart went out to them. But did my hand reach out to them? No, this girl stayed home, stayed warm, and prayed for them. Of course, I came up with all kinds of reasons—okay, excuses—not to act.

- Their power will come on any minute now.
- Surely they have whatever they need.
- I don't want to be a nuisance.
- Our driveway is *solid ice*.
- I'd feel foolish knocking on their door.
- What would I take? Blankets? Hot chocolate?

As usual, I missed the point. The act of charity, the loving gesture, was what mattered. Not the gift itself, but the giving. God gently but firmly showed me the error of my thinking. *If you want to be closer to Me, Liz, then you need to give like Me.*

This is why we study God's Word. Not just to understand it, not just to meditate on it. God wants us to *do it*. He calls us to act. And He gives us the power to do so.

Most of us would rather not be called a *do-gooder*—a person who tries to help those in need yet does so in a way that's naive, annoying, useless, even prideful. But we all want to *do good*. This verse shows us the difference between doing a good thing and doing a God thing.

Do not withhold good . . . *Proverbs 3:27*

I sure wish this translation put a more positive spin on things, like "Do everything you possibly can" (ERV) or simply "Do good" (EXB). That's what the original Hebrew gives us—a single word, *towb,* which means "beautiful, pleasant, good, agreeable."

Yet most versions urge us, "Don't hold back good" (NIrv) and "Never walk away" (MSG). That's because our flawed human nature prods us to keep rather than give, hoard rather than share, and withhold rather than extend. Whether it's money, time, or the place we call home, we guard them as if they're ours instead of blessings from God, entrusted to us so we can care for others.

It's not that we're selfish or greedy or controlling. Oh no. We just want to make sure people have earned the right to whatever we give them.

. . . from those to whom it is due, . . . *Proverbs 3:27*

Due? Sounds like these people not only "deserve it" (NLT), but they're also "entitled to it" (CJB). Why? Because they "need help" (EXB), and we're meant to provide it by the Lord's design.

God considers us worthy so we can consider others worthy.

God blesses us so we can bless those around us.

There's nothing here about requiring those in need to prove it, take a number, fill out this form, or stand in this line. God's Word says just the opposite. Don't hold back. Share. Do good. Be generous. Give with joy, because "God loves a cheerful giver."[1]

The verse that follows this one in Proverbs makes it clear God is talking about giving something tangible, something material: "Do not say to your neighbor, 'Come back tomorrow and I'll give it to you'—when you already have it with you,"[2] when "the money's right there in your pocket" (MSG).

Open your hand. Hold it out. Help.

. . . *when it is in your power . . . Proverbs 3:27*

This isn't Jim Carrey strutting around the set of *Bruce Almighty,* lip synching to "I've Got the Power." This is you, filled with the Holy Spirit, quietly, humbly serving God by giving to others "whenever you possibly can" (GNT).

Wrapped inside the original Hebrew phrase is the word *el* for "God," and *yad,* meaning "hand." God puts the power in our hands, saying, "Go. Give." The power comes from on high, and so does the provision.

We may sing, "He's got the whole world in His hands,"[3] but it's more than that, dear friend. We're His hands to the world. As The Message puts it, "Your hand is God's hand for that person."

When is it *in your power?* Right now.

... to act. *Proverbs 3:27*

That's right. Just "do it" (asv). Reach out your hand. Since "it is within your power" (voice), then by all means "help" (net). The Hebrew here is an active verb, telling us to "accomplish, do, make." Not merely think about, but act upon.

We must give, or we risk losing all the joy of having. By the power and conviction of the Holy Spirit, He teaches us to say no to clutching our money with both hands and say yes to sharing our time, our money, our energy, our prayers, and our hearts with those in need.

As Paul wrote, "Let us not become weary in doing good, for at the proper time we will reap a harvest if we do not give up."[4]

Lord Jesus,
help me not give up,
become weary, or opt out.
Instead, teach me
to give generously,
to give joyfully,
to give continually.
Everything that's ours
is Yours, Lord.
Please remind me of that.
Often.

One Minute, One Step

Doing good means letting go.

Look around and select an item you enjoy yet think might be helpful to another person. Something you are willing to give away. Even better, something you're *not* eager to part with. Put this item in your car to deliver to the nearest charity shop or donation center. If you're away from home just now, write down a possession you can load in your car the next time you walk through the door.

Do not withhold good from those to whom it is due,
when it is in your power to act.

Proverbs 3:27

24

Apples to Apples

Like apples of gold in settings of silver
is a ruling rightly given.

PROVERBS 25:11

Autumn, with its brilliant blue skies and crisp air, means an abundance of apples at the Higgs house. Apple cider, freshly pressed. Apple cobbler, hot from the oven. Apples dipped in caramel and rolled in nuts. Yes, please.

Still, an apple plucked fresh from the tree is the best treat of all.

Bill swears by Golden Delicious. Lilly's a Gala girl. Matt likes to sink his teeth into a nice green Granny Smith, and Beth loves Pink Ladies. Me? I'm a McIntosh woman to the core. It's all about the flavor, texture, and juiciness. You no doubt have a favorite too.

But our "golden apple" (ERV) in Proverbs is appealing for a different reason.

Like apples of gold . . . *Proverbs 25:11*

We're told these are "precious" (CEV) and valuable, pleasing to the eye "like a design of gold" (GNT). Though the Hebrew word *tappuach* simply means "apple," in this verse it's made out of *zahab*—pure gold. This proverbial fruit has been admired, sought after, and savored through the centuries. Like wisdom. Like honor. Like truth.

It's also beautifully displayed.

. . . in settings of silver . . . *Proverbs 25:11*

Whether it's a "silver tray" (HCSB) or something "inscribed with silver" (JUB), it's lovely to look at, "as beautiful as gold apples in a silver bowl" (NCV). Biblical commentator Matthew Henry suggests this "ornament of the table" was well known in Solomon's time.[1] Maybe that's why the writer of Proverbs compared this dish of golden apples to the equally impressive fare we find in the second half of the verse.

. . . is a ruling rightly given. *Proverbs 25:11*

"The right word spoken at the right time" (ICB) truly is delicious. When an idea is "well-expressed" (GNT) and "skillfully spoken" (NET) by someone who knows what she's talking about, everyone looks around with a sense of satisfaction. They smile at one another and then nod their heads in happy accord. After all, "timely advice is lovely" (NLT) and serves a useful purpose.

Instead of argument, agreement. Instead of dissent, consent. All because of a "word aptly spoken" (OJB).

Sensitivity is everything when it comes to choosing the words we speak. And that's where I usually blow it. Standing in our wedding reception line, I gushed to a single friend, "You'll be next!" *So thoughtful, Liz.* No wedding guest wants to be reminded that she came alone, especially if she longs to be married and has no current prospects.

Another embarrassing example. A friend who is deaf and incredibly gifted at reading lips spoke at our local Christian school. Knowing how rambunctious primary students can be, I asked her, "Were the kids quiet for you?" She said with a straight face, "Oh, they were very quiet." *Real sharp there, Liz.*

Instead of being like apples of gold in a setting of silver, my words are often more like stale popcorn in a striped paper bag. That's why this is my constant prayer: "Let the words of my mouth and the meditation of my heart be acceptable in your sight, O LORD, my rock and my redeemer."[2]

Our words can do more than simply make people feel better. They can make people's lives better. When God calls us to "speak up for those who cannot speak for themselves, for the rights of all who are destitute,"[3] He's urging us not to take the easy route—keep quiet, say nothing—but to speak the words that need to be spoken. To write a letter to the editor, to post the facts on social media, to make a phone call to the mayor's office, to send an e-mail to local broadcasters. To give a voice to those who have no voice.

"A well-spoken word at just the right moment" (VOICE)? That's a solid-gold apple, my friend.

Heavenly Father,
You know how much I love words.
Yet only Your Word
has the power to make us new.
When I look for ways
to encourage others,
may I turn to Your Word first.
When I look for ways
to make a difference,
may I trust Your Word
to light the way.

One Minute, One Step

Today share a golden apple.

Who has served as a mentor or role model to you? A teacher, a grandparent, a friend? Write this special person a note of encouragement, polishing your thoughts until they shine with God's favor. Perhaps a few well-chosen words on a greeting card or a fruit basket with a personal message is more your style.

Whatever method you choose, make it beautiful, make it meaningful, make it now.

Like apples of gold in settings of silver
is a ruling rightly given.

PROVERBS 25:11

25

Silver Is the New Gray

Gray hair is a crown of splendor;
it is attained in the way of righteousness.

PROVERBS 16:31

When my first gray hair appeared in my thirties, it was well hidden beneath Clairol's Nice'n Easy Natural Medium Ash Blonde, my hair color of choice back in the day.

In my forties I avoided the salt-and-pepper look by going paprika—okay, more like Light Auburn from L'Oréal (because I'm worth it). I celebrated turning fifty in proper biblical fashion, since "in this Year of Jubilee everyone is to return to their own property."[1] But when I gave my hair back to God, I discovered—eek!—it was mostly silver with some dark blond in the back. Who knew?

Now that my silver hair has been on display for more than a decade, I count this proverb as one of my favorites, as do many of our sisters. Whatever your age, beloved, you'll find something of value here.

Gray hair is . . . *Proverbs 16:31*

Let's be honest. Gray is gloomy. Think rain clouds, battle-ships, dingy sheets, sadness. And a translation like "hoary head" (ASV) doesn't improve matters. That's why I favor "silver-haired" (NKJV) or, even more appealing, "silvery" (OJB). Silver is shiny. Think gleaming jewelry, sterling teapots, newly minted coins, regal crowns. Not to mention those women blessed with "hair that is turning white" (NLV), as pure and lovely as freshly fallen snow.

Of course, our hair color doesn't matter *one bit* in any spiritual sense. It's the maturity, the ripe "old age" (DRA) we've reached that's truly a gift from God. Although my husband turned silver in his late twenties, gray hair is primarily "the splendor of the old."[2] It's years in the making. Hard won. Well deserved. Impressive.

. . . a crown of splendor; . . . *Proverbs 16:31*

How delicious that phrase is! When our silver hair appears, it's a crown of "glory" (ASV), "honor" (CJB), "dignity" (DRA), and "beauty" (AMPC). Rather than seeing this sign of maturity as a negative, we need to see it as a "mark of distinction" (MSG) that's natural and good and "glorious" (NIrV).

As it happens, in our look-younger-at-all-costs culture, many of us dye our silver crowns rather than polish them. Heaven forbid we should look old! One mature woman clucked her tongue at me and said, "Honey, you are aging yourself ten years with that gray hair." (It was really hard not to snap back, "And you, honey, are fooling no one with your hair color not found in nature!" But I didn't. Honest.)

Meanwhile, guess who's excited about our silver crowns? Women under thirty, judging by the positive comments I've received whenever I'm out and about. Wild, right? Could be they're happy to see older women take what God has given them and run with it. Why not? It's just hair. My daughter insists mine is the color of starlight. And I love, love, *love* not having to touch up my roots every two weeks. Saves a bunch of time, effort, and money.

If you color your hair, no need to apologize. We all come to our own conclusions about these things. I simply couldn't miss this opportunity to say if you're considering taking a leap of faith, go for it. You have lots of naturally silver sisters who've paved the way.

> . . . it is attained in the way of righteousness.
> *Proverbs 16:31*

This crown that God bestows on us, this indicator of wisdom and maturity, cannot be bought. Nor is there a shortcut. "It is earned" (ERV) by experiencing God's constant presence and "found" (KJV) through seasons of faithfulness, which He alone makes possible.

For all of us, at any age, here's the truth:

We're righteous because of His righteousness.

We're worthy because He is more than worthy.

We're crowned because He is our mighty King.

We're going the right way because His is the only way.

This "path" (CEB) of righteousness may not always be a straight line—the Hebrew word, *derek,* is often translated "journey"—but if we're walking with the Lord, we're definitely moving in the right direction. And it helps if we take our sense of humor with us.

One predawn morning I woke up from a dream and found myself sitting on the floor. It took me a moment to figure out what had happened. The risky combination of a nylon nightgown, silky smooth sheets, and a narrow twin bed meant that when I'd turned over in my sleep, I'd slid out of bed and onto the plush carpet of my hotel room.

At first I giggled. The bed was low to the floor, so I'd not hurt anything. But then I tried to stand and realized I was in trouble. Every surface was either too soft, too slippery, or too wobbly to provide any support. With my new bionic left knee and a bum right one, I didn't dare try to kneel. To make matters more interesting, I was alone in a foreign country, the hotel phone was far from my reach, and it was four o'clock in the morning.

I confess, I got a little teary for a minute. Then I looked out the window at the dark sky filled with stars and decided the wisest move I could make was to ask God to help me.

Please, Lord.

His answer came at once. *The windowsill.*

Yes! If I could somehow make my way across the room to the broad wooden sill, I might have enough leverage to pull myself to my feet. Getting there was fairly amusing, since rolling was my only option. So roll I did, laughing all the way. The slinky nightgown turned out to be an asset—less friction on the carpet. Within minutes I was standing, no worse for wear and wide awake.

This is why I love maturity. If I'd been twenty years younger, I would have simply stood up and gone back to bed. End of story. Instead, I started the day reaching out to God, and a joy-filled memory was born. It's the best way—really the only way—to live.

However many years we're given on this earth, let's aim to be "God-loyal" (msg), seeking His strength to lead "a righteous life" (esv), realizing what matters most is being right with Him.

Heavenly Father,
thank You for giving me
another day, another month, another year.
Help me see silver hair
as yet another gift from Your loving hands.
Not a dreaded sign of old age,
but a welcome sign of Your
timeless wisdom.

One Minute, One Step

Relax. Recharge. Renew.

Whatever your hair color, comb it for a full sixty seconds. (Brushing a wig or hairpiece counts too.) Enjoy the sensation of your tingling scalp or the calming motion of the repetitive brushstrokes. Now think of something that makes you smile. *Ah.* Feel better?

Gray hair is a crown of splendor;
it is attained in the way of righteousness.

PROVERBS 16:31

26

Here Comes Trouble

When pride comes, then comes disgrace,
but with humility comes wisdom.

PROVERBS 11:2

*P*ride isn't *always* a bad thing, is it? We call children our
pride and joy, we sing the national anthem because we're
proud of our country, and even God's Word says of Israel, "I will
make you the everlasting pride and the joy of all generations."[1]

But pride in ourselves? In our good works? In our virtues?
That kind of pride will get us in major hot water. The Lord makes
this abundantly clear, especially in the Old Testament, where the
word *pride* appears more than sixty times and almost never in a
positive light. God promises His people, "I will break down your
stubborn pride"[2] and "put an end to the arrogance of the haughty."[3]

Time to gird our loins and prepare to be humbled. Not

because we're bad and deserve to be punished, but because God is good and wants what is best for us. Always.

When pride comes, . . . Proverbs 11:2

Not *if*, not *maybe*, but *when*. Pride comes to us all. It's only a matter of time and place. Whether we're puffed up and "swelling" (AMPC) or trying to hide behind false humility, pride is one of the dark sides of human nature.

I believe every sin has pride at its root. It's counted among the classic list of seven deadly sins—pride, wrath, greed, gluttony, sloth, envy, lust. Yet pride may be the underlying reason we get angry when we don't get our way, overspend when we want to impress others, overeat because we think our bodies are no one's business but ours, waste time because we care only about our own schedules, want what others have so we can be their equal, and let our libido run wild because our sexual needs must be met even if others are hurt in the process.

One translation of this verse begins "First comes pride" (CJB). Too right. At the very start of the human race, pride convinced our first Bad Girl of the Bible, Eve, that she had to have a bite of that forbidden fruit. The snake appears to have started the conversation, but it was Eve's pride that convinced her to act. "When the woman saw that the fruit of the tree was good for food and pleasing to the eye, and"—here we go—"also desirable for gaining wisdom, she took some and ate it."[4]

This wasn't merely about feeding her appetite or holding something beautiful in her hands. This was about trying to gain wisdom from a source other than God. This was "I want that, I deserve that, and I'm going to have that." This was "Look how clever I am now and how much smarter I'll be after I eat this!"

One bite and Eve's pride-happy party was over. "The LORD God said to the woman, 'What is this you have done?'"[5] *Yikes.*

... then comes disgrace, ... *Proverbs 11:2*

The outcome is inevitable. "Disgrace follows" (HCSB) pride, and "shame is not far behind" (VOICE). The Message nails it: "The stuck-up fall flat on their faces." We're standing on a pedestal of our own making one minute and then sweeping up what's left of it the next. Such "dishonor" (NASB) isn't easily overcome, and the sense of "emptiness" (AMPC) lingers.

The problem with pride is the *I* in the middle.

In my young adult years, I thought the Bible was an anti-quated book of rules, a boring list of thou-shalt-nots. Only after I'd come to the end of myself did I finally understand that God's path is not just the best path; it's the only path that leads to peace with Him, now and forever. My testimony in a sentence? "He lifted me out of the slimy pit, out of the mud and mire; he set my feet on a rock and gave me a firm place to stand."[6]

I am a case study in the dangers of being prideful and am beyond grateful for His mercy.

... but with humility ... *Proverbs 11:2*

Humble people are "modest" (ERV) and "down-to-earth" (MSG). They think about others before themselves and about God before anyone else. They willingly "renounce self" (AMPC). They're "not proud" (NIrV), they're "lowly" (YLT), and they do life with "meekness" (WYC).

Humility isn't something we can manufacture on our own. It's what happens when we walk humbly with God,[7] noticing how big His footprints are compared to ours. Humility means allowing Him to teach us rather than our insisting we know everything.

It's better to be humble than to be humbled, "pruned or chiseled by trial" (AMPC). But whatever it takes—and for some of us that means a sharp set of pruning shears or a very heavy chisel—the result is more of God, less of us. *Yes.*

Here's the best part: our patient God is the One who does the pruning and chiseling. He is the One who helps us grow into the image of His Son. Who better to wield the shears or chisel than the One who loves us completely?

What's next? You guessed it.

. . . comes wisdom. *Proverbs 11:2*

If "wisdom comes to those who are not proud" (NIrV), then "it's wiser to be humble" (CEV). The two—humility and wisdom—are intertwined. Only when we are humble are we teachable. Only when we are empty can we be filled. Only when we see God alone as our source of wisdom can we truly become wise.

One of the joys of wisdom is that it "stays" (ERV). Pride can be dismantled in a heartbeat, but no one can undo the wisdom God gives to those He prunes, chisels, and loves.

Heavenly Father,
You squeeze more truth
into a handful of words
than I could manage
in a lifetime of talking.
I hear what You are saying
about pride,
especially mine.
And I understand what You mean
about humility
and my lack thereof.
Please prune, Lord.
And chisel.

One Minute, One Step

**Make the first move. Forgo pride,
and embrace humility.**

Think of someone you have wronged, hurt, or offended.
Even if you did so without meaning to, she or he deserves
an apology. Pray first. Then send this person a text, an
e-mail, or a brief note if only to say, "We need to talk." Get
the conversation started. It's time.

*When pride comes, then comes disgrace,
but with humility comes wisdom.*

PROVERBS 11:2

27

Tomorrow, Tomorrow

Do not boast about tomorrow,
for you do not know what a day may bring.

PROVERBS 27:1

This verse is a simple note of caution, reminding people not to brag about tomorrow. Really, who does such a thing?

You do, Liz.

When the Lord pokes me like that, using the double-edged sword of His Word, I know I'm in trouble. Even so, good news is on the horizon. Because with God there is always good news.

Do not boast about tomorrow, . . . *Proverbs 27:1*

What does that look like? We might forward our overloaded schedule to friends, asking for prayer but secretly hoping they'll be impressed with all we're doing. Or we could spend endless hours organizing our calendars in color-coded glory instead of taking care of what needs to be done right now. Or we might blithely tell people about our plans for next year, confident all will come to pass precisely as planned.

Now here comes this verse urging us to "never brag" (ERV) or "brashly announce" (MSG) our plans for tomorrow. It's best if we "do not talk much" (NLV) about, let alone "glory over" (WYC), what we have in mind for next week, next month.

Are we to live only for today? Forget about the future?

We've all seen T-shirts and coffee mugs proclaiming *carpe diem,* meaning "seize the day." It's interesting that only the first part of the famous statement is typically quoted. The rest is *quam minimum credula postero,* which translates as "put very little trust in tomorrow."[1] That last bit? It's the heart of this verse from Scripture.

For years we've sung "Don't stop thinking about tomorrow."[2] God says just the opposite: Stop thinking about tomorrow. Stop bragging about it, putting your trust in it, and counting on your future to unfold the way you expect it to.

This is why:

> . . . for you do not know what a day may bring.
> *Proverbs 27:1*

We think we know what tomorrow holds. Just look at our Blue Sky weekly planners or the calendars on our phones with something noted for every hour. Do this. Go there. Make that. It's in ink; it's a done deal; it's a sure thing. But the truth is, we "have no idea" (ERV) what's going to happen tomorrow.

People may break their promises, leaving us high and dry. A change in the weather may undo our plans. A check we're depending on might not arrive in the mail. Our car may refuse to start. The school nurse could send a text, telling us to pick up our sick child in the next fifteen minutes.

Or we could get a phone call with the worst news imaginable.

Admit it. We "don't know the first thing about tomorrow" (MSG) and can't predict "what will happen between now and then" (GNT).

A thousand years after Solomon wrote this verse in Proverbs, Jesus offered the same wisdom: "Therefore do not worry about tomorrow, for tomorrow will worry about itself. Each day has enough trouble of its own."[3] And James reminded us, "Now listen, you who say, 'Today or tomorrow we will go to this or that city, spend a year there, carry on business and make money.' Why, you do not even know what will happen tomorrow. What is your life? You are a mist that appears for a little while and then vanishes."[4]

There's a sobering thought. We might not even be here tomorrow. Every day on our planet more than 150,000 people die.[5] That's more than 6,000 people an hour. More than 100 people a minute. I'm not trying to discourage you, just pointing out the obvious. Tomorrow isn't guaranteed to anyone.

My father was a good person, a man of high principles and deep integrity. But he was not a man who believed in God or read the Bible or prayed for his family. As much as it grieves me to admit this, after his ninety years on this earth, he didn't choose to be counted among God's children.

Still, I am not a woman without hope. If my father gave his heart to Christ in the twilight hours after his stroke, I will be the first to leap with joy when I see him in heaven. It won't be my father's goodness that will have opened that door. It will be God's goodness, God's kindness, God's mercy.

That's why God asks us to trust our tomorrows to Him. To embrace the promises in His Word: "There is surely a future hope for you, and your hope will not be cut off."[6] He wants us to rest in Him, knowing He is in charge and holds our future safely in His loving hands.

Joshua trusted the Lord implicitly and so told his people, "Consecrate yourselves, for tomorrow the LORD will do amazing things among you."[7] Not *you* will do amazing things; the Lord will do them. When we think about tomorrow, we're not to focus on our ability to make things happen but on God and what He is able to accomplish, which is "immeasurably more than all we ask or imagine."[8]

His Word reminds us, "Each day brings its own surprises" (CEV). They could be good surprises. Something life changing might happen tomorrow. Something fabulous that's not on your list, not on your radar, yet God has already put it in motion. James gave us the right way to handle tomorrow: "You ought to say, 'If it is the Lord's will, we will live and do this or that.' "[9]

Having a list of things to do is fine if we seek God's leading when we make those plans and hand them over to Him at the start of each day. God has tomorrow covered according to His perfect will. Our job? Celebrate today. *Carpe diem,* if you will. As the psalmist said, "The LORD has done it this very day; let us rejoice today and be glad."[10]

We're rejoicing, Lord. And trusting You—today, tomorrow, and forever.

Lord Jesus,
I give all my tomorrows
to You. Right now.
They're already Yours.
I just need to acknowledge that.
To smile at the future,
knowing it's in Your hands.
To rejoice that tomorrow
is a finished work for You.

One Minute, One Step

Seize the next sixty seconds.

Since we can never be sure what tomorrow will hold, imagine the next minute is your last before you step into heaven. What vital message do you want to leave for the world? What *one thing* do you want everyone to know? The clock is ticking. Grab a pen and paper, or record it on your smartphone. Go.

Do not boast about tomorrow,
for you do not know what a day may bring.

PROVERBS 27:1

28

She Still Speaks

She speaks with wisdom,
and faithful instruction is on her tongue.

PROVERBS 31:26

When the most famous woman in the book of Proverbs "opens her mouth" (ESV), she doesn't fill the air with mere sound. She fills it with wisdom.

To be honest, I'm not intimidated by the fact that she "selects wool and flax and works with eager hands"[1] or that she "considers a field and buys it."[2] Every woman has her unique set of skills. But this business about the words she speaks? Oh my.

She speaks with wisdom, . . . *Proverbs 31:26*

Look, I am a woman who speaks a lot—basically from the moment I open my eyes until I finally close them at night. Hour by hour I toss out opinions, advice, ideas, observations, random thoughts—all that. You can be sure if it's on my mind, it's on my lips.

Now the time has come to ask some hard questions. Are the words I speak "skillful and godly" (AMPC)? Are they "sensible" (CEV)? Do I have anything "worthwhile to say" (MSG), or am I simply talking my way through life? Because when our Proverbs 31 sister speaks, "her mouth is full of wisdom" (CEB). She offers something worth hearing.

If you struggle as I do with an overabundance of words, don't lose heart. Here's what else this admirable woman is dishing out.

. . . and faithful instruction . . .
Proverbs 31:26

She's offering what's known in Hebrew as *torah*—"direction, instruction, law." Not a bunch of rules, but the law of "mercy" (JUB), "kindness" (KJV), and "grace" (GNV). She's teaching her family about God's loyalty, faithfulness, and loving-kindness, and she's glorifying God with her words. As a mother, she surely talks about what's for dinner and whose turn it is to wash the dishes. But the most important thing she talks about is God's love.

. . . is on her tongue. *Proverbs 31:26*

She's also not shy about sharing her faith. God's mercy is always on the tip of her tongue: "I will declare that your love stands firm forever, that you have established your faithfulness in heaven itself."[3]

For those of us with the gift of gab, this really is good news.

We don't have to stop talking. We just need to weave the truth of God's love in and through our conversations as the Spirit leads.

When we study God's Word, it shapes our words. When we seek His mercy, we can speak with mercy. When we focus on Him, we may help others see Him more clearly.

I'm grateful for the supportive friends who walked beside me when I was a new Christian and showed me what it means to be a follower of Christ. But even they were surprised when I announced that God was calling me to a distant mission field. Really distant: Indonesia.

True, I'd been a believer only six months, after a wild and woolly decade as a Really Bad Girl. I also had no husband at the time, no college degree, and little knowledge about Indonesia other than how to find it on a globe. Still, Christians are called to "go into all the world."[4] Shouldn't I go too?

When I threw myself at a mission board, certain they'd be thrilled to take me, the director was very kind. He listened, nodded, took notes. And then he said the last thing I expected: "I'm sorry, Liz. But . . . no."

My heart sank. I thought if I simply offered to go, they'd say, "Great! Sign here."

After he explained why I wasn't the best candidate for foreign missions, he assured me, "Liz, you're already well versed in a culture most Christians know little about."

I knew where this was going. He meant my old life. My Bad Girl life.

His voice softened. "Do you know the story of the woman at the well? After she met Jesus, she went back to the town where everyone knew her sordid story, and she told them about Jesus. That's what you need to do."

"You mean tell the people I used to hang out with?" My cheeks grew hot even thinking about it. "The people I partied with? The men I slept with? *Those* people?"

"You speak their language," the director reminded me. "And you love them."

I could feel Indonesia slipping away from me as I pictured the faces of old friends who knew *way too much* about me. People as lost and confused as I'd once been. People who needed to know Jesus.

"Never fear." The missions director placed a gentle hand on my shoulder and escorted me to the door. "God will take care of Indonesia."

So I went back to Louisville and told my story. Soon one co-worker came to know Jesus. Then another. Then a third. Who knew? God knew. And He never forgot my heart for Indonesia.

Twenty years after my no-go with the mission board, I was standing in my publisher's booth at a Christian booksellers gathering. The guy in charge of international rights pulled me aside and said, "Liz, please meet our new friend from World Harvest."

A tiny woman with thick black hair looked up, her face radiant. "I am in the process of translating three of your books into my country's language."

"Wonderful!" I beamed at her. "What country might that be?"

She beamed back. "Indonesia."

Oh my. Only God could manage such a thing. And He wasn't finished. When I shared my experience at an evangelism conference, one of the guest speakers approached me. "Liz, would you like to speak in Indonesia?"

My heart skipped a beat. *Would I?!* I could barely get out the
words. "Wh-who would my audience be?"

"Women," she assured me. Then smiled. "Missionaries."

Lord Jesus,
the tenderness of Your mercy overwhelms me.
You miss nothing. You care about everything.
You answer my deepest longings, according to
Your perfect will and Your perfect timing.
You alone know my mission field, Lord.
Help me serve You
wherever You send me.

One Minute, One Step

❦

**Speak His wisdom until
you know it by heart.**

Write this proverb several times on a piece of paper. Recite
it aloud if you're in a good place to do so. Then carry it
with you for the next twenty-four hours and commit it to
memory. Of the many verses we've walked through, Proverbs 31:26 might be the most life changing of all.

*She speaks with wisdom,
and faithful instruction is on her tongue.*

PROVERBS 31:26

29

Green-Eyed Girl

A heart at peace gives life to the body,
but envy rots the bones.

PROVERBS 14:30

I was a member of a professional association for just two weeks when I attended their national convention. Since my name badge didn't sport a single special ribbon, people barely glanced at me. Alone in my hotel room, I ended each day in tears, feeling inadequate and overwhelmed. I told myself I wasn't envious (heaven forbid!). I was simply . . . uh, discouraged.

Years passed. Doors began to swing open. Ribbons dangled from my name badge, and people smiled in my direction. Soon I found myself dealing with a different set of feelings. *How come she's moving ahead faster than I am, Lord? Why did they honor her instead of me?* I wasn't jealous, of course. I was merely . . . uh, disappointed.

The awful truth revealed itself one rainy morning when I received an announcement from a colleague who'd been blessed with an opportunity I was convinced should have been mine. I tossed her letter across the room in an angry huff. "It's not fair, Lord!"

His response was swift. *Have I called you to succeed, Liz, or to surrender?*

I knew the answer. Even so, jealousy and envy were alive and well in my jade-green heart. When I reached out to my writing and speaking sisters—women who love and serve the Lord—I discovered they, too, wrestled with this issue. One said, "I understand competition in the secular marketplace. But I grieve over it in the body of Christ. What are we doing, setting one person's work above another's, if not absorbing the world's way of doing things?"

Her words echo the apostle Paul's: "For since there is jealousy and quarreling among you, are you not worldly? Are you not acting like mere humans?"[1] Yes, we are. For all of us who struggle with envy, here are some stepping-stones toward victory.

A heart at peace . . . *Proverbs 14:30*

That's surely our goal: to have "a tranquil heart" (ASV) and "a calm and undisturbed mind" (AMPC). Healing begins when we acknowledge that envy is a sin: "If you harbor bitter envy and selfish ambition in your hearts, do not boast about it or deny the truth."[2]

Humble admission is the best antidote for prideful ambition. So is avoiding comparison. When Peter fretted over John's place in Jesus's ministry and asked, "Lord, what about him?" Jesus answered, "What is that to you? You must follow me."[3]

Patience also helps us defeat envy. Many a career or ministry has collapsed under too much, too soon. It's better to embrace the tasks we've been given rather than longing for something bigger, better, or faster.

Success can be a dangerous word for a follower of Jesus, unless by *success* we mean "pleasing God." He alone makes a truly satisfying life possible. His brand of success isn't money or fame or power. It's *love* for one another. By definition, "Love is patient, love is kind. It does not envy, it does not boast, it is not proud."[4]

It's also wise to befriend your supposed rival. As one of our sisters explained, "A woman was brought in on a fast-track executive management program at my corporation. At our first meeting I thought, 'Well, here's my rival.' Then I heard God say, 'She is smart, energetic, and sharp—just like you. You could become best buddies.'" And that's just what happened.

Whenever we're feeling overlooked or passed over, we can lift up our heads and celebrate with others. Sending an e-mail or text on the spot will chase away those negative feelings. If we "rejoice with those who rejoice,"[5] we won't have time to feel sorry for ourselves.

Doing the right thing is always the right thing to do. We're happier and healthier for it, and so are others around us.

. . . gives life to the body, . . . Proverbs 14:30

If envy is deadly, then generosity of spirit "is life and health" (AMP). It not only "revives the body" (NET) at the cellular level; it can also "add years to one's life" (VOICE). This is God's Word talking, not the latest Mayo Clinic newsletter. As the Lord affirms, "It's healthy to be content" (CEV) and seldom wise to want more.

. . . but envy rots the bones. Proverbs 14:30

Behind every successful woman is a host of sacrifices we never see. The truth? We're seldom jealous of all the work a person does. We just want the favorable outcome. Envy "can eat you up" (CEV) almost "like a cancer" (ERV). Instead of a peaceful heart, you'll have a "wasting away of the bones" (NLV), a kind of spiritual osteoporosis.

The path to true success is bathed in the light of genuine humility. "Humble yourselves, therefore, under God's mighty hand, that he may lift you up in due time."⁶ The right time. His time.

Dear Lord,
I know envy and jealousy
have no place in the
hearts of those You love.
Please forgive me
when I'm tempted to grumble over
how much You have blessed others,
forgetting the many ways
You have kindly blessed me.
Give me the grace
to wholeheartedly rejoice
and celebrate Your gifts,
fully alive in them.
Help me walk the path
You've chosen for me.
Content. At peace.
Giving thanks.

One Minute, One Step

Count your blessings.

List all the things you're grateful for that you can name in sixty seconds. The order doesn't matter. The gratitude does.

A heart at peace gives life to the body,
but envy rots the bones.

PROVERBS 14:30

30

Step into the Light

Whoever conceals their sins does not prosper,
but the one who confesses and renounces them finds mercy.

PROVERBS 28:13

Since this verse talks about confessing our sins, I'll go first. I used to indulge in a certain guilty pleasure, especially while traveling. After buying my stash from an airport shop, I inhaled it on the plane, hoping no one was looking. Not dark chocolate, not illicit drugs, but something equally addictive: romance novels.

Love stories are one thing. These were something else. Not uplifting Christian novels. The other kind. Pretty flowers on the cover, innocent-sounding titles, but the content definitely didn't qualify as "whatever is true, whatever is noble, whatever is right, whatever is pure."[1]

A happily married woman, I convinced myself that reading

such stories was harmless. I wasn't fantasizing about other men, wasn't hurting anyone, wasn't breaking any laws.

Really, Liz? God's Word tells us, "Have nothing to do with the fruitless deeds of darkness, but rather expose them. It is shameful even to mention what the disobedient do in secret."[2]

The romance novels I chose—dozens upon dozens—were definitely fruitless, producing nothing healthy in my spiritual life or in my marriage. And they were decidedly shameful. I did everything I could to hide them, reading in bed at night with my back toward my husband, or reading in public with a quilted book cover masking the subject matter.

> Whoever conceals their sins does not prosper, . . .
> *Proverbs 28:13*

When we need to hide what we're doing, we need to ask ourselves why. God's Word makes it clear that, for "those who hide their sins" (CEB), "it will not go well" (NLV). Not only are you sure to be found out; you also "will be a failure" (CEV).

Forgive me if I'm stepping on your toes here. It's not my intent to judge you, only to show you how much Jesus loves His daughters. So much so that He stands ready to rescue us the moment we realize we're drowning and cry out for help.

For me, that desperate moment came during a Christian women's conference in Georgia nearly twenty years ago. During the closing minutes of the Saturday night session, the speaker offered an invitation to come forward and have a heart-to-heart conversation with the Lord.

Here's the thing: I was the speaker who offered that invitation.

The worship leader sat behind me, softly playing music on a keyboard, while I encouraged our sisters in Christ to take a brave step of faith and come forward to pray. Some came alone, others in pairs, often weeping. The empty floor in front of the stage began to fill with women seeking His forgiveness.

Your turn, Liz.

My words faded into silence. The prompting in my heart wasn't audible, but I knew it was the Lord, and I knew what He wanted me to do.

Now, Liz. Go.

. . . but the one who confesses and renounces them . . .
Proverbs 28:13

That's what God was asking of me: to "give them up" (CEV). A woman who "stops doing wrong" (ERV), who "abandons" (CJB) her sin and leaves it behind is a woman set free. The Lord knows we can't do this alone, so He stands ready, willing, and more than able to help us overcome our weaknesses through the power of His Spirit. "Look to the LORD and his strength; seek his face always."[3]

I put down the microphone with shaking hands, nodded at the musician to keep playing, and then stepped down and knelt on the floor. *Forgive me, Lord. Help me, Lord.* My whispered confession poured out. So did my tears, hot with shame.

As I sensed His mercy washing over me, my cheeks grew cooler, and my breathing eased. I was left with nothing but gratitude and a clear sense of what had to be done when I got home.

But what to do *now*? A thousand women had watched their speaker abandon the platform to pray. *What must they be thinking?* I stepped back onstage and faced the audience. Turned out, they weren't thinking about me at all. They were kneeling. Everywhere. On the floor, in the aisles, in front of their chairs.

It wasn't my invitation they responded to. It was God's.

"I have come into the world as a light, so that no one who believes in me should stay in darkness."[4] He wants us to live in the light of His love, and He asks us to leave our dark deeds behind. The first step is the hardest: admitting we're in trouble. But, oh, the freedom we encounter when we discard our secret sins and step into His light!

Conviction comes when the Holy Spirit reveals that our lives aren't lining up with God's truth. Confession is next, as we name our sin and ask His forgiveness. Contentment follows when we make the needed changes, depending on His strength alone.

Every woman who turns to Him with confession on her lips discovers grace in His hands.

. . . finds mercy. *Proverbs 28:13*

You won't find judgment or condemnation. You'll find "compassion" (AMP). The one who turns away from her sin "gets another chance" (TLB). I am living proof, and so are millions of your sisters. If your confession is real, His forgiveness is even more so.

Heavenly Father,
thank You for not leaving me
in darkness and shame,
for showering me with grace,
for showing me the way out.

One Minute, One Step

Come clean with God.

Wash your hands, working up a good lather, and then rinse, watching the soapy water swirl down the drain. This is what Jesus does for us spiritually: He washes away our sins so completely that nothing is left behind but our clean hearts.

Now, if you have some hand lotion, rub it into your skin, enjoying the sweet scent and remembering the fragrance of His grace that covers every inch of you.

Whoever conceals their sins does not prosper,
but the one who confesses and renounces them finds mercy.

PROVERBS 28:13

31

Straight On till Morning

In all your ways submit to him,
and he will make your paths straight.

PROVERBS 3:6

Our children were eight and ten when I told them about my past. My sin-filled, gin-soaked, not-a-nice-girl past.

The soft April light warmed our sunporch that Saturday afternoon as the kids and I sat together, their little knees pressed against mine. I knew if I reached for their hands, they'd worry—*uh-oh, Mom is up to something here*—so I simply made sure I had their full attention.

"You know I'm speaking at church tomorrow, right?"

Two heads bobbed up and down. Pink-cheeked, blue-eyed, wavy-haired Lilly and her older brother, Matt, with his sweet, round head and earnest expression. So innocent, so trusting.

I tried to smile but failed miserably. Tried to start over, but the words wouldn't come. The thing is, I'd shared my testimony for years. Churches, youth rallies, women's groups. But confessing the same facts with my children sitting in the front pew, looking up at their mother—*their mother*—while she said words like *pot* and *speed* and *cocaine*, suddenly felt like a really bad idea.

That's why I had to prepare them. *Had to.*

But the words I'd chosen seemed lame, inadequate. How could I help them understand my wild and foolish past—a litany of sins committed and forgiven long before I met and married their grace-giving father?

I was also nervous about what they would think of their mother. Would they still respect me, still trust me, still obey me, still love me? More to the point, would they still love Jesus?

I looked at each of them in turn and then silently begged for the right words.

"Tomorrow morning," I began, "I'll share some of my faith journey as part of the service. It's just five minutes. But I want you to hear what I'm going to say first. Okay?"

Matt frowned. "Is it something bad?"

"Sort of." I swallowed. "You see, before I met Jesus . . ." My voice trailed off. How could I possibly say this? "Before I met Jesus, my life was . . . my life was . . ."

Nothing came out. *Please, Lord.*

Then Lilly said in a small voice, "Sad?"

Yes. Overwhelmed, I sank deeper into the couch. "My life was *very* sad. But not anymore."

I began to unwrap my story, sharing only a few necessary

details, mindful of their tender ages. "It's the end of the story that matters, not the beginning," I assured them. "Because of Jesus, we're forgiven and made new. Isn't that amazing?"

Yes, they agreed. Amazing.

I'm grateful to say they still love me. Far better, they still love God. They also avoided following in their mother's footsteps when they became teenagers—my greatest fear of all. Instead, they told their friends, "Oh, my mom did all that stuff ages ago. Whatever."

I'd blown the cool factor. Perfect.

If you're wondering how much of your own past might be appropriate to share with others, here's my take. Be gentle. Be honest. And trust God completely to guide you.

In all your ways . . . *Proverbs 3:6*

Hard to get around that word *all.* Utterly inclusive. Nothing left out. "Everything you do" (GNT) pretty much covers it.

. . . submit to him, . . . *Proverbs 3:6*

The Hebrew word *yada* means "to know," which suggests a broader meaning than "submit." We are to care more about knowing the Lord than knowing ourselves. To "remember" (GNT), "acknowledge and recognize" (AMP) Him. To "think about what he wants" (ERV) and discover everything we can about His character, His attributes, His nature.

This is what God is waiting for us to grasp: *If you knew Me, you would trust Me.*

. . . and he will make your paths straight. Proverbs 3:6

No *maybe* here. A promise. A guarantee. "He's the one" (MSG) who will do this.

The truth? God is in control whether we acknowledge His sovereignty or not. We do not *make* Him Lord. He *is* Lord. The moment we accept that reality, the very second we bend our hearts and knees to His power and might, we find our loving God has already taken us by the hand and is leading us in the right direction.

This is a kind and compassionate God. He doesn't wind us up like toys or pull our strings like puppets. He promises, "I will instruct you and teach you in the way you should go; I will counsel you with my loving eye on you."[1]

He sees us, loves us, counsels us, teaches us. He creates a perfect path for each of us and then helps us walk forward, picking us up when we stumble. He walks before us and behind us. He is on our right hand and on our left. He provides and protects. He guides and directs.

God promises He will "help you go the right way" (ERV), which is His way. That's the only way you want to walk. Not because you aren't smart enough to chart your own course, but because you're smart enough to know His course is the best one for you.

God doesn't say, "My way or the highway." God says, "Come, follow me."[2] His love and mercy make walking in tandem with Him possible.

Our paths aren't meant to be straight in a literal sense, like ruled lines. After all, it's the unexpected curves, the bends in the road that keep us on our toes and make the whole trip worthwhile. He promises to "guide you on the right paths" (HCSB) and "keep you on track" (MSG), no matter how many potholes appear between here and heaven. My Bad Girl years were no surprise to God, and they didn't disqualify me from serving Him. Whatever you stumbled over in your past isn't an issue for the One who knows your future.

When you follow God, you never have to worry where you're going or who will clear the path of debris or how long the journey will take. Look to the One who knows you, the One who loves you, the One who leads you. He charts the path. He lights the path. He *is* the path.

Your part, my friend, is to keep walking, keep trusting, and keep looking up.

Lord Jesus,
I want to trust You in all things,
not just some things.
Help me learn from You.
Help me lean on You.
Help me let go of my stubborn need to control.
Help me understand that
loving You with all my heart means
trusting You with all I was and am
and ever will be.

One Minute, One Step

Some things only God can plan.
And some things you can plan.

Choose what you're going to wear tomorrow, from under-garments to clothing, jewelry to shoes, and place them in the front of your closet or on a chair. In the morning you'll be grateful for fewer decisions to make, fewer things to slow you down.

You'll also be reminded of a loving God who has laid out your day with far greater care and precision, knowing what each minute will hold. Sleep well tonight, beloved. Tomorrow is in good hands. His hands.

In all your ways submit to him,
and he will make your paths straight.

PROVERBS 3:6

Study Guide

A re you ready to take the truths you've found in these verses from the ancient book of Proverbs and apply them to your thoroughly modern life? This Study Guide is for you! Whether you use this section on your own or in a small-group setting, the questions here will help you dig deeper into Scripture and learn more about the One who offers us His wisdom, knowledge, and understanding free for the asking.

You'll want a handy place to record your answers—tablet, notebook, computer, whatever you choose—as together we continue down the path He has prepared for us.

VERSE 1: MORNING BY MORNING

The path of the righteous is like the morning sun,
shining ever brighter till the full light of day. PROVERBS 4:18

1. Do you see yourself as righteous? What do Romans 1:17; Romans 4:3; and 2 Corinthians 5:21 tell you about the meaning of *righteousness*?
2. In what ways is the Lord your Source of light and life? What encouragement do you find in Psalms 27:1; 36:9; 56:13; and John 8:12?

❧ VERSE 2: WISDOM'S SOURCE

For the LORD gives wisdom;
from his mouth come knowledge and understanding. PROVERBS 2:6

1. Describe what *wisdom* means to you. How is it different
   from facts and information? From knowledge and understanding? According to Ephesians 1:17, what is the source
   and goal of wisdom? How would growing in wisdom help
   you and those around you?

2. Deuteronomy 31:12 describes two important benefits of
   listening to God's Word spoken publicly. What do you
   think could happen if someone stood before your church
   and read the Word of God with unbridled passion for a full
   hour and without adding a single word of his or her own?

❧ VERSE 3: WEIGH IN

A person may think their own ways are right,
but the LORD weighs the heart. PROVERBS 21:2

1. Think about a less-than-ideal interaction you had with
   someone recently. At any point did you try to justify your
   actions, either to the other person or to yourself? What
   insight does Proverbs 16:2 offer regarding the dangers of
   trusting our own perceptions in such situations? And what
   guidance do Ephesians 4:15 and 4:25 provide for next
   time?

2. In the "One Minute, One Step" prompt for this verse, I
   asked you to prepare an envelope of cash to share with
   someone in need. If you've done something like this before,

what was the outcome? If you haven't ever handed money to a stranger, what are your expectations? What does 1 Chronicles 29:17 tell us about David's attitude and the people's attitude toward giving? How does that align or contrast with your thoughts and desires?

 ## VERSE 4: COVER UP

Hatred stirs up conflict,
but love covers over all wrongs. PROVERBS 10:12

1. Imagine living in a peaceful home where love always triumphs. Now, how would you describe your childhood home? Your current home? What do the words of Jesus recorded in John 14:27 and 16:33 tell us about the source of peace? And what does Paul suggest in Romans 12:18 about our role in the matter?

2. Forgiveness is often hard to extend to others and even harder to receive. Why might that be the case? What do Matthew 6:14–15 and Luke 6:37 teach us about God's forgiveness? How does His forgiveness enable us to forgive others?

 ## VERSE 5: NO TELLING

A gossip betrays a confidence,
but a trustworthy person keeps a secret. PROVERBS 11:13

1. In what situations are you tempted to gossip? Though Proverbs 20:19 begins the same way Proverbs 11:13 does, the second half of 20:19 offers additional advice. How could you put that idea into action?

2. We find even more pointed counsel in 1 Timothy 3:11, aimed specifically at women. Do you think women struggle with gossip more than men do? What factors might contribute to any seeming differences in this area? If you need to be a better secret keeper, how will you seek God's help?

✳ VERSE 6: WE ALL FALL DOWN

Pride goes before destruction,
a haughty spirit before a fall. PROVERBS 16:18

1. When has pride plunged you headlong into disaster? What sort of fall did you experience, and what did God teach you in the process?
2. Proverbs 29:23 shows us how God can use even our foolish pride to good effect. And what assurance do Psalm 138:6 and James 4:10 offer?

✳ VERSE 7: WITH THIS RING

Her husband has full confidence in her
and lacks nothing of value. PROVERBS 31:11

1. Just as some women have a hard time not gossiping, others among us have a hard time not spending. On a scale of one to ten—one being terrible and ten being terrific—how trustworthy are you when it comes to explaining how you spend your money? To whom are you accountable? What caution does 1 Timothy 6:10 give us?
2. In the story I shared about our diamond shopping experience, the central issue wasn't money. It was integrity. It was

trustworthiness. When have you faced a similar temptation? What promise and what warning do you find in
Proverbs 10:9?

 ## Verse 8: Bloom On

The fruit of the righteous is a tree of life,
and the one who is wise saves lives. PROVERBS 11:30

1. In your circle of friends, who resembles a "tree that bears
   life-giving fruit" (TLB)? What do they do for others that
   stands out? Do their righteous deeds inspire you, or do they
   intimidate you, and why? What might God be calling you
   to do in this season of your life?
2. When we plant the seed of the gospel in someone's heart,
   amazing things can happen. How does Matthew 13:31–32
   encourage you? And what does 1 Corinthians 3:6 remind
   us about the growth process of any seeds we plant?

 ## Verse 9: Fool's Gold

The way of fools seems right to them,
but the wise listen to advice. PROVERBS 12:15

1. Mr. T used to say, "I pity the fool!" What wise advice does
   Proverbs 14:7 offer concerning fools? What would you
   consider the single most foolish thing a person could do?
   What makes you say that?
2. I wrote, "One path I've learned to avoid is gathering lots of
   opinions." Do you agree or disagree? What if you sought
   only God's counsel? How would you do it, and how could
   you be certain you heard from Him?

VERSE 10: HEAVY LIFTING

Anxiety weighs down the heart,
but a kind word cheers it up. PROVERBS 12:25

1. What does anxiety look like in your life? Are you more inclined to be anxious about the past, the present, or the future? What does 1 Peter 5:7 tell us to do with our anxious thoughts? And how could you do that, exactly?

2. I shared some encouraging texts from a friend that kept me going when the going got tough. What kind words do *you* need to hear regularly? Who is most likely to speak those words? According to 2 Thessalonians 2:16–17, who is our most dependable source of encouragement?

VERSE 11: TONGUE-TIED

Those who guard their lips preserve their lives,
but those who speak rashly will come to ruin. PROVERBS 13:3

1. Psalm 34:13 reveals two things *not* to do or say, and Psalm 37:30 tells us two things we *should* be saying. Consider how these four things are to shape our conversations. Can a believer park somewhere in the middle of those options? Why or why not?

2. On page 63 I offer this simple suggestion before opening our mouths: Stop. Look. Listen. Pray. Which of these steps come naturally to you? And which do you need to work on? What wisdom do you find in James 1:19? Are you slow or quick to anger? If quick, how could you put on the brakes?

VERSE 12: HOME DECONSTRUCTION

The wise woman builds her house,
but with her own hands the foolish one tears hers down.
PROVERBS 14:1

1. Ask a family member or close friend, "What speaks love
   to you?" Did his or her answer surprise you? How does it
   spur you to change the way you interact with this person?
   Note some specific instructions you find in Romans 12:10;
   2 Corinthians 13:11; and 1 Peter 3:8. Choose one you
   would like to do more consistently.

2. In what ways have you decorated your home—literally or
   figuratively—to put Christ and His Word at the center?
   Read Deuteronomy 6:6–9 and consider how you could
   put those truths into practice in your own household.

 VERSE 13: LESS IS BEST

Better a little with the fear of the LORD
than great wealth with turmoil. PROVERBS 15:16

1. Answer the two questions I posed at the start of the reading:
   What do you want more of in your life? And what do you
   want less of? Consider the counsel you find in Proverbs 11:28
   and 23:5. How have those truths played out in your life?

2. What's your strategy for pushing back against today's
   more-more-more message? Is there a verse you turn to? A
   specific experience you call to mind? What kind of riches
   should we pursue, as God's Word explains in Romans
   11:33; Ephesians 1:7; and Colossians 1:27?

VERSE 14: HOW WE ROLL

Commit to the LORD whatever you do,
and he will establish your plans. PROVERBS 16:3

1. Are you a planner? Is your calendar crammed with details from now until next Christmas? Or do you take life as you find it, not looking too far ahead, not writing things down? What are the advantages of each method? The disadvantages? How can we best honor the Lord with our calendars, whatever our personal approach to planning?

2. Look at the blessing David requested in Psalm 20:4. How do these words align with God establishing your plans? Practically speaking, how can you roll all your plans, your hopes, your dreams onto His shoulders? What insight does Psalm 20:7 provide?

VERSE 15: WORTH THE WAIT

Hope deferred makes the heart sick,
but a longing fulfilled is a tree of life. PROVERBS 13:12

1. Do you consider yourself a hope-filled person? Would people who know you agree or disagree? On what do you base your hope, and how does it sustain you? What does Hebrews 10:23 challenge us to do, and why?

2. What unfulfilled longing remains in your life? How do you keep hoping when nothing seems to be happening? Read 1 John 3:2–3. What promise does Christ offer? How will that help you wait and trust while you're living in the here and now?

Verse 16: Soul Food

Gracious words are a honeycomb,
sweet to the soul and healing to the bones. Proverbs 16:24

1. Nutritionists urge us to keep track of every bite of food we take. But what does Jesus teach in Matthew 15:10–11 about the importance of what goes into our mouths versus what comes out? And what further illumination does Romans 10:9–10 offer on this subject?

2. The first part of Ephesians 4:29 tells us what *not* to do. Come up with a practical way you could remind yourself to think before you speak so your words will be sweet and not bitter. What guidelines do you find in the second half of Ephesians 4:29?

 ## Verse 17: Smart Money

How much better to get wisdom than gold,
to get insight rather than silver! Proverbs 16:16

1. You could spend twelve years going to school, another four years attending college, three more years seeking a master's degree, and several more earning a doctorate, yet all your worldly knowledge would be no match for God's wisdom. Proverbs 23:23 suggests you can buy wisdom. What might that actually mean? If you can't purchase wisdom, how can you acquire it, according to 1 Corinthians 1:28–30?

2. What direction does Hebrews 13:5 provide concerning money? And how does Philippians 4:12 challenge you regarding contentment? If you consider yourself content,

how did you get there? If not, how will you begin moving in
that direction?

 VERSE 18: GOOD MEDICINE

A cheerful heart is good medicine,
but a crushed spirit dries up the bones. PROVERBS 17:22

1. Your sense of humor is a vital part of your personality. What
   makes you laugh? Jokes? Sight gags? Clever wordplay? Do
   you tend to laugh at people? At circumstances? At yourself?
   Are you a giggler? A howler? Something in the middle?
   What does Psalm 126:2 suggest is the source of our deepest
   laughter, our greatest joy? How has this proved true in your
   life? If laughter is lacking at your house, what can you do to
   restore a sense of joy?

2. Even those of us who love to laugh can suffer from depression, clinical or otherwise. Read Psalm 143 as if the enemy
   mentioned is depression itself. What are the various ways
   the psalmist, David, described his thoughts, feelings, and
   experiences? Which of them could describe moments in
   your life? What prescription did David offer? And what's
   the next step you might need to take as you seek relief?

 VERSE 19: BEST-LAID PLANS

Many are the plans in a person's heart,
but it is the LORD's purpose that prevails. PROVERBS 19:21

1. Whether you make plans on the spur of the moment or have
   a three-year planning calendar, when and how do you

consult the Lord before proceeding with your plans for the
day? If that's not something you typically do, what changes
might you experience in your life if you did seek God first?
How can you remind yourself to do that daily? And what
specific steps will you take?

2. Since we know the Lord's purpose prevails, how do the
following verses help us understand His purpose in our
lives: Exodus 9:16; 2 Corinthians 5:5; and Philippians
2:12–13? Is God's purpose for your life different from His
purpose for everyone else's, or is it the same? What makes
you say that?

Verse 20: Tower of Power

The name of the LORD is a fortified tower;
the righteous run to it and are safe. Proverbs 18:10

1. Draw a picture of a strong tower, perhaps one you've seen
in person or in a movie. Imagine you are hiding inside it,
seeking refuge. Now, beside the walls of this tower, write its
many qualities: formidable, impenetrable, unshakable—
whatever you need your tower to be. How is God all these
things to you? What comfort and assurance do you find in
Psalms 5:11; 9:9; 18:2; 59:16; and 61:3?

2. On pages 114–15 I suggest three ways we might run to His
name. Describe a time when you spoke His name and were
rescued, a time when you opened His Word and found
refuge, and a time when you sought His church and
discovered a true sanctuary. What does being safe mean
to you? What benefit of safety does Psalm 4:8 mention?

VERSE 21: IN THE SPOTLIGHT

The human spirit is the lamp of the LORD
that sheds light on one's inmost being. PROVERBS 20:27

1. In what ways does the reality of God's seeing and knowing everything about you, even your innermost secrets, impact how you think about yourself? And how you think about God? Psalm 18:28 says "my God turns my darkness into light." When and how has He done that in your life?

2. Who do you know that's filled with the light of the Lord? Describe her spiritual life, those things you've learned or observed about her. What does she say or do to let His light shine through her? How does she serve as a role model for you? Finally, what do all the mentions of light in 2 Corinthians 4:6 reveal about our source of light?

 ## VERSE 22: LOOKING GLASS

As water reflects the face,
so one's life reflects the heart. PROVERBS 27:19

1. What words come to mind when you think of your body? Your face? Your hair? Since God finds you beautiful as is, what will it take for you to agree with Him? Though a mirror may reflect what we look like to others, it doesn't reveal what we look like to God. What qualities does God see in your heart that He loves?

2. According to His Word, God is most pleased by our obedience. What do these verses teach us about obedience: Deuteronomy 8:6; 1 Kings 8:58; 2 Corinthians 9:13; and

2 John 1:6? Define what *obedience* means to you. How does our obedience—or lack thereof—reflect what's in our hearts?

✦ VERSE 23: DO GOOD

Do not withhold good from those to whom it is due,
when it is in your power to act. PROVERBS 3:27

1. If you're quick to help others, list all the reasons you might be compelled to do so, digging deep to find every possible motive. If you're less eager to be of service, list some honest reasons why that is the case. According to John 14:26, what motivates and enables us to do good? Therefore, what would it take to become a better doer?

2. What's the hardest thing for you to give others? Time? Money? Effort? Possessions? Expertise? Affection? And what's easier for you to give? What important truth does Matthew 6:1–4 teach us about giving to those in need? Practically speaking, how might that truth impact your future giving?

✦ VERSE 24: APPLES TO APPLES

Like apples of gold in settings of silver
is a ruling rightly given. PROVERBS 25:11

1. Our words can either be delicious and nutritious or sour and unsatisfying, like biting into a shiny apple and discovering it's rotten to the core. What good fruit can we produce, according to Hebrews 13:15? And as we learn in John 15:4, how is such fruit bearing possible?

2. When did someone offer you just the right word at the right
time? What positive impact did it have? Now recall when
the wrong word at the wrong time had a negative impact.
What did you learn from that experience? How can you be
ready to hand out golden apples of praise in any season?

 ## VERSE 25: SILVER IS THE NEW GRAY

Gray hair is a crown of splendor;
it is attained in the way of righteousness. PROVERBS 16:31

1. Let's talk about gray hair for a moment. When you see other
people with gray, silver, or white hair, is your reaction
positive, negative, or neutral, and why? How do you feel
about your own hair turning gray? More to the point, how
do you feel about growing older? What favorable light does
this verse shine on maturity? In what ways does God's
promise in Isaiah 46:4 encourage you?

2. According to Matthew 21:32, John the Baptist taught
people the "way of righteousness," which the tax collectors
and prostitutes embraced and the chief priests and elders did
not. According to Isaiah 26:7–8, what *is* the way of righteousness? Does our age either hinder or facilitate our access
to that path, and why?

 ## VERSE 26: HERE COMES TROUBLE

When pride comes, then comes disgrace,
but with humility comes wisdom. PROVERBS 11:2

1. As I stated in the text, "I believe every sin has pride at its
root." Do you agree or disagree? What examples from your

life could you offer to support your opinion? What does
Proverbs 21:4 say? And what does God have in store for
the proud, according to Psalm 31:23; Proverbs 3:34; and
Proverbs 16:5?

2. God shows us how to avoid disgrace—the very opposite
   of His grace—by being humble. The essence of humility
   is beautifully stated in Philippians 2:3–8. Read the
   verses aloud, and then list all the characteristics of
   humility. How can we hope to become such a person,
   to become like Christ, as this New Testament passage
   instructs us?

 ## Verse 27: Tomorrow, Tomorrow

Do not boast about tomorrow,
for you do not know what a day may bring.
Proverbs 27:1

1. What does the axiom "Seize the day, put very little trust in
   tomorrow" mean to you personally? In what ways does it
   align with scriptural truth? And how might it differ? What
   are some of the dangers of boasting about tomorrow? If
   you've experienced a downside to such boasting, what did
   you learn in the process?

2. Read Proverbs 31:25. The first half of the verse tells us how
   to "dress for success," so to speak. The second half of the
   verse shows us how to handle tomorrow and the next day
   and the next. Rather than run away from the future or run
   headlong into the future, what does God's Word tell us to
   do? Why is that a wise plan? How have you found that
   approach to be of value in your life?

Verse 28: She Still Speaks

She speaks with wisdom,
and faithful instruction is on her tongue. Proverbs 31:26

1. On a scale of one to ten—one being a very quiet woman and ten being a constant talker—how would you score yourself? And how might your friends score you? This verse from Proverbs addresses the quality of a woman's words rather than the quantity, but how might it encourage those of us who are tens to speak less and say more? And how might it encourage the ones among us to become bolder and speak up? What encouragement do you find in Acts 28:31 and 2 Corinthians 3:7–12?

2. If you've had a sense of God calling you to share His good news, where has it taken you, and what have you discovered on your journey, whether around the world or around the block? How do John 4:41 and Acts 20:2 demonstrate the benefits of sharing our words rather than remaining silent?

Verse 29: Green-Eyed Girl

A heart at peace gives life to the body,
but envy rots the bones. Proverbs 14:30

1. Are jealousy and envy the same thing, or do they have distinct meanings to you? In what situations are you most likely to struggle with envy? If you've learned to overcome jealous thoughts and feelings, describe your path to victory. If you're still a work in progress, how will you be ready the next time that green-eyed girl raises her hand?

2. Humility is one of the recommended antidotes for jealousy. Gratitude is another. According to 1 Corinthians 15:57 and 1 Thessalonians 5:18, what are two reasons we are to be thankful? For your "One Minute, One Step" exercise, I encouraged you to list as many things as possible in sixty seconds. Which did you run out of first: time or things you're grateful for? Why might that be the case?

 ## Verse 30: Step into the Light

Whoever conceals their sins does not prosper,
but the one who confesses and renounces them finds mercy.
Proverbs 28:13

1. Oh, the lengths to which we will go to hide what we don't want others to see! Yet what do Proverbs 15:3 and Jeremiah 16:17 make clear? Though others may be fooled, God is not. Why is that a good thing?

2. It's embarrassing to admit our weaknesses, our mistakes, and especially our sins. But when we confess and repent, the grace and mercy God pours over us is worth it all. How have you found that to be true in your walk with the Lord? What direction does Hebrews 4:16 offer?

 ## Verse 31: Straight On till Morning

In all your ways submit to him,
and he will make your paths straight. Proverbs 3:6

1. In the end God wants our whole hearts. He wants us to know Him, obey Him, trust Him, follow Him, submit to

Him. What does the word *submit* mean to you? And how do the following verses help you further grasp the meaning: Job 22:21; Ephesians 5:21; and Hebrews 12:9?

2. Now that we've spent many hours together in His Word and in His presence, which verse from Proverbs has spoken most to your heart, and why? And in what specific ways has His light brightened your path as you look ahead? Ephesians 1:18 sums up my heart's desire for you: "I pray that your hearts will be flooded with light so that you can understand the confident hope he has given to those he called—his holy people who are his rich and glorious inheritance" (NLT).

Heartfelt Thanks

Whether you've read several of my books over the years or this is the first time we've met, my gratitude goes to you first and foremost, dear friend. You are the reason I write. I can never thank you enough!

I'm also deeply in debt to my editorial team: Laura Barker, Carol Bartley, Sara Fortenberry, Rebecca Price, and Matthew Higgs. Once again you did a stellar job of lighting my path and keeping me on track. As for my silver-haired husband, Bill Higgs, I'm even more in love with you now than I was the day we said, "I do." I still do, sweet man. Today, tomorrow, and forever.

Finally, many thanks to Melody Henderson for her fine proofreading, to Angie Messinger for her speedy typesetting skills, to Rose Decaen for proofing our final pages, to Karen Sherry for a delightfully designed interior, and to Kelly Howard for a book jacket that gleams with warmth and light.

Notes

Walk with Me
1. Proverbs 4:11
2. Proverbs 6:9
3. Proverbs 4:24
4. Proverbs 6:23

1. Morning by Morning
1. Galatians 5:22–23
2. Psalm 145:13
3. Romans 3:22
4. John 8:12

2. Wisdom's Source
1. Genesis 1:3
2. Isaiah 55:11, NIrV
3. David A. Graham, "Rumsfeld's Knowns and Unknowns: The Intellectual History of a Quip," *Atlantic,* March 27, 2014, www.theatlantic.com/politics /archive/2014/03/rumsfelds -knowns-and-unknowns-the -intellectual-history-of-a-quip /359719/.
4. Isaiah 55:9
5. James 1:5

3. Weigh In
1. Judges 21:25, NASB
2. 1 John 3:19–20
3. Hebrews 4:12

4. Matthew 25:45
5. Daniel 5:27

4. Cover Up
1. 1 John 4:11
2. Further information on the Hebrew and Greek words referenced in this book can be found in Francis Brown, *The New Brown-Driver-Briggs-Gensenius Hebrew and English Lexicon* (Lafayette, IN: Associated Publishers and Authors, 1980), and Robert L. Thomas, ed., *New American Standard Exhaustive Concordance of the Bible with Hebrew-Aramaic and Greek Dictionaries* (Nashville, TN: Holman, 1981).
3. Psalm 64:3
4. 1 Corinthians 13:5
5. 1 Corinthians 13:7
6. 1 Peter 4:8

8. Bloom On
1. Psalm 92:14
2. Psalm 1:3
3. Ezekiel 17:24, CEB
4. Luke 8:15

5. James 5:19–20
6. Ezekiel 36:26

9. Fool's Gold
1. James 5:13
2. Psalm 37:5
3. Proverbs 27:6
4. Proverbs 18:2

10. Heavy Lifting
1. Deuteronomy 31:6
2. John 14:27
3. Psalm 94:19

11. Tongue-Tied
1. Proverbs 12:18
2. Colossians 3:16
3. 1 Thessalonians 2:4
4. John 16:13

12. Home Deconstruction
1. Matthew 7:25

13. Less Is Best
1. Ephesians 3:18
2. Exodus 15:11
3. Hebrews 12:28
4. Ecclesiastes 2:11

14. How We Roll
1. Proverbs 16:9
2. Hebrews 3:1
3. Luke 1:37, NASB
4. Luke 1:37, NCV
5. Luke 1:37, KJV

15. Worth the Wait
1. Psalm 130:5

2. Psalm 42:5
3. Psalm 42:5
4. Psalm 27:14
5. Psalm 102:1
6. Psalm 84:12
7. "Revolution of Tenderness; Pope Francis's TED talk: the full transcript and video," Quartz Media LLC, https://qz.com/968 060/pope-franciss-ted-talk -the-full-transcript-and -video/.

16. Soul Food
1. 1 Thessalonians 5:11
2. Psalm 90:17, NKJV
3. Psalm 19:10
4. Ezekiel 3:3

17. Smart Money
1. Oscar C. A. Bernadotte, "I'd Rather Have Jesus," Timeless Truths, http://library.time lesstruths.org/music/Id _Rather_Have_Jesus/.
2. Matthew 25:21

18. Good Medicine
1. John 15:11
2. Job 8:21

19. Best-Laid Plans
1. Luke 14:28
2. Psalm 20:4
3. Romans 12:2
4. Psalm 31:14
5. Hebrews 13:8

6. Revelation 21:4
7. Psalm 33:11

20. Tower of Power
1. "Word Study: YHWH (God)," Chaim Bentorah: Biblical Hebrew Studies, September 10, 2012, www.chaimbentorah .com/2012/09/word-study -yhwh-god/.
2. Psalm 46:1
3. Matthew 9:12

21. In the Spotlight
1. Genesis 2:7
2. Matthew Henry, *Matthew Henry's Commentary on the Whole Bible,* www.bible studytools.com/commentaries /matthew-henry-complete /proverbs/20.html.
3. Job 32:8
4. 1 John 1:9, ASV
5. Proverbs 13:9

22. Looking Glass
1. Ecclesiastes 3:11
2. See Exodus 38:8.
3. 1 Samuel 2:3
4. 1 Corinthians 13:12
5. James 1:23–25, NLT
6. Philippians 2:15, CJB

23. Do Good
1. 2 Corinthians 9:7
2. Proverbs 3:28
3. Writer unknown, "He's Got the Whole World in His

Hands," Songs for Teaching, www.songsforteaching.com /religious/biblesongs/samson anddelilah/hesgotthewhole world.htm.
4. Galatians 6:9

24. Apples to Apples
1. Matthew Henry, *Matthew Henry's Commentary on the Whole Bible,* www.bible studytools.com/commentaries /matthew-henry-complete /proverbs/25.html.
2. Psalm 19:14, ESV
3. Proverbs 31:8

25. Silver Is the New Gray
1. Leviticus 25:13
2. Proverbs 20:29

26. Here Comes Trouble
1. Isaiah 60:15
2. Leviticus 26:19
3. Isaiah 13:11
4. Genesis 3:6
5. Genesis 3:13
6. Psalm 40:2
7. See Micah 6:8.

27. Tomorrow, Tomorrow
1. Latin Discussion, http://latin discussion.com/forum/latin /translating-quam-minimum -credula-postero.24368/.
2. Christine McVie, "Don't Stop," copyright © 1977, Universal Music Publishing Group.

3. Matthew 6:34
4. James 4:13–14
5. "World Birth and Death Rates," Ecology, www .ecology.com/birth-death -rates/.
6. Proverbs 23:18
7. Joshua 3:5
8. Ephesians 3:20
9. James 4:15
10. Psalm 118:24

28. She Still Speaks
1. Proverbs 31:13
2. Proverbs 31:16
3. Psalm 89:2
4. Mark 16:15

29. Green-Eyed Girl
1. 1 Corinthians 3:3
2. James 3:14
3. John 21:21–22
4. 1 Corinthians 13:4
5. Romans 12:15
6. 1 Peter 5:6

30. Step into the Light
1. Philippians 4:8
2. Ephesians 5:11–12
3. 1 Chronicles 16:11
4. John 12:46

31. Straight On till Morning
1. Psalm 32:8
2. Matthew 4:19

Additional Bible Versions

About the Author

Liz Curtis Higgs loves the Lord, loves His Word, and loves her sisters in Christ. She is the author of more than thirty books, with 4.6 million copies in print, but what she cares about most are the women who hold her books in their hands and the ones seated in her audiences, first row to last.

In her best-selling nonfiction series—*Bad Girls of the Bible, Really Bad Girls of the Bible, Unveiling Mary Magdalene,* and *Slightly Bad Girls of the Bible*—Liz breathes new life into centuries-old stories about the most famous women in scriptural history, from Bathsheba to Jezebel to Rahab.

In *The Girl's Still Got It,* Liz offers a twenty-first-century take on the book of Ruth, dishing out meat and milk, substance and style, in a deeply personal journey with Naomi and Ruth. *The Women of Christmas* invites readers to experience the season afresh with Elizabeth, Mary, and Anna, just as *The Women of Easter* walks through Holy Week with Mary of Bethany, Mary of Nazareth, and Mary Magdalene. And in *It's Good to Be Queen,* Liz escorts readers inside the courts of King Solomon, where the queen of Sheba shows us all how to be bold, gracious, and wise.

A seasoned professional speaker and Bible study teacher, Liz has toured with Women of Faith, Women of Joy, and Extraordinary Women. She has spoken for seventeen hundred other women's conferences, which has taken her to all fifty states in the United States and fifteen foreign countries, including Thailand, Portugal, South Africa, Japan, Ecuador, and New Zealand.

Liz is married to author Bill Higgs, PhD, who serves as director of operations for her speaking and writing office. Louisville, Kentucky, is home for Liz and Bill, their grown children, and their twin tabby cats, Boaz and Samson. Liz is quick to confess she's a lame housekeeper, a marginal cook, and a pitiful gardener. Even so, home is her favorite place to land.

Follow Liz's free online Bible study on www.LizCurtisHiggs .com, and find her on www.Facebook.com/LizCurtisHiggs, on www.Twitter.com/LizCurtisHiggs, on www.Instagram.com/Liz CurtisHiggs, on www.Vimeo.com/LizCurtisHiggs, and on www .Pinterest.com/LizCurtisHiggs.

LET HIS *Truth* FIND A *Home* IN YOUR *Heart*

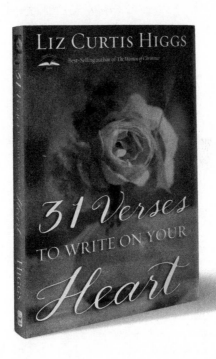

Liz Curtis Higgs offers a deeper, richer understanding of thirty-one treasured verses, and creative ways to keep them in your heart forever. With a Study Guide included, *31 Verses to Write on Your Heart* is a daily devotional and a small group Bible study, wrapped in a lovely gift book.

LEARN THE TRUTH
ABOUT GOD'S GOODNESS FROM THE BIBLE'S BAD GIRLS

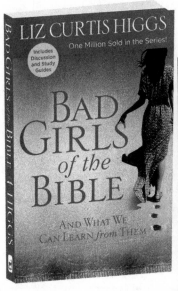
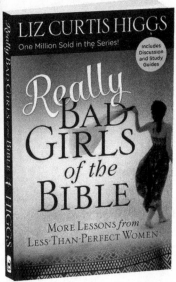

One million readers have taken a walk on the wild side with Former Bad Girl, Liz Curtis Higgs, and her eye-opening blend of contemporary fiction and biblical commentary. Laced with humor and heartfelt self-disclosure, Liz's unique brand of "girlfriend theology" has helped women of all ages experience God's grace anew.